Hang-Gliding from Helicon

Hang-Gliding from Helicon

New and Selected Poems
1948–1988

Daniel Hoffman

Louisiana State University Press
Baton Rouge 1988

Copyright © 1974, 1975, 1976, 1977, 1978, 1979, 1980, 1981, 1982, 1983, 1984, 1986, 1987, 1988 by Daniel Hoffman
All rights reserved
Manufactured in the United States of America

10 9 8 7 6 5 4 3 2 1

Designer: Albert Crochet
Typeface: Linotron
Typesetter: Focus/Graphics
Printer: Thomson Shore, Inc.
Binder: John H. Dekker & Sons, Inc.

The author acknowledges the publishers of the books from which the poems herein have been selected: Yale University Press—*An Armada of Thirty Whales* (New Haven, 1954), copyright © 1954 by Yale University Press, renewed 1982 by Daniel G. Hoffman; Oxford University Press—*A Little Geste* (Oxford, 1960), copyright © 1952, 1955, 1957, 1958, 1959, 1960 by Daniel G. Hoffman, *The City of Satisfactions* (Oxford, 1963), copyright © 1961, 1962, 1963 by Daniel Hoffman, *Striking the Stones* (Oxford, 1968), copyright © 1963, 1964, 1965, 1966, 1967, 1968 by Daniel Hoffman, and *Broken Laws* (Oxford, 1970), copyright © 1966, 1968, 1969, 1970 by Daniel Hoffman; and Random House—*The Center of Attention* (New York, 1974), copyright © 1970, 1971, 1972, 1973, 1974 by Daniel Hoffman. Thanks are due to the editors of the following publications, in which some of the poems in "Hang-Gliding from Helicon" previously appeared: *Boulevard, Hampden-Sidney Poetry Review, Negative Capability, New-England Galaxy, New England Review, New Republic, Ontario Review, Panoply, Parnassus, Pennsylvania Gazette, Shenandoah,* New York Times, and *Yale Review.* "Witnesses" and "At Don's Garage" previously appeared in *The American Poetry Review.* "Folk Tale," "Himself," "High Society," and "Essay on Style" first appeared in *The Hudson Review.* "At the Roman Wall" first appeared in *Poetry.* "Stop the Deathwish! Stop It! Stop!" and "Ode to Joy" first appeared in *The Southern Review.* "The Battle of Hastings" and "Fontaine-les-Dijon Revisited" first appeared in *Poetry Northwest.* The poem "Mark Twain, 1909" appeared originally in *The New Yorker.* "Last Lynx" first appeared in *The Georgia Review.*

LIBRARY OF CONGRESS CATALOGING-IN-PUBLICATION DATA

Hoffman, Daniel, 1923–
    Hang-gliding from Helicon: new and selected poems, 1948–1988
Daniel Hoffman.
      p.   cm.
    ISBN 0-8071-1452-9 (alk. paper).   ISBN 0-8071-1453-7 (pbk. : alk. paper)
    I. Title
PS3515.02416H3 1988
811'.54—dc19   87-32993
                                                                                                    CIP

The paper in this book meets the guidelines for performance and durability of the Committee on Production Guidelines for Book Longevity of the Council on Library Resources. ∞

Publication of this book has been supported by a grant from the National Endowment for the Arts in Washington, D.C., a federal agency.

This book is for
LIZ

Contents

The Poem   1

From *An Armada of Thirty Whales* (1954)

Incubus   5
The seals in Penobscot Bay   6
An armada of thirty whales   8
At Provincetown   9
That the pear delights me now   10
The clams   12
Old Bug up there   13
On the extinction of a species   14
The larks   14
The voice of the woodthrush, played at half speed   15
Auricle's oracle   15
Ephemeridae   16
I dreamt my love a-dying lay   17

From *A Little Geste* (1960)

In the Beginning   21
The Hermit of Cape Rosier   23
Exploration   25
Safari   26
Flushing Meadows, 1939   27
In the Days of Rin-Tin-Tin   28
Awoke into a Dream of Singing   28

From *The City of Satisfactions* (1963)

A New Birth   31
A Meeting   32
The Chosen   34
The Unchosen   35
Climbing Katahdin   37
In That High House   38
Saint-Apollinaire   39
Dijon   40

Vezelay   41
1956   43
A Letter to Wilbur Frohock   45
Gestures   47
Mi-Carême   48
The Pursued   50
The City of Satisfactions   51
The Great Horse Strode Without a Rider   54
As I Was Going to Saint-Ives   56

From *Striking the Stones* (1968)

The Way It Is   59
There   60
Testament   61
In the Pitch of Night   62
In Provence   63
Instructions to a Medium, to be transmitted to the shade of W. B. Yeats, the latter having responded in a séance held on 13 June 1965, its hundredth birthday   64
Words for Dr. Williams   66
A Visitation   67
On the Industrial Highway   68
Shaking the President's Hand   69
Crop-Dusting   69
The Peaceable Kingdom   70
Open Letter, Returning a Questionnaire Unanswered   72
Breathing Purely   73
Banished   74
Moving Among the Creatures   75
Signatures   76
At Evening   77
Far-Off Light   78
Inviolable   79
First Flight   80
A Solitary   81
The Companion   81

'He was the first who had returned'   82
The Last Arrival   83
'When my wiser brother'   84
The Way He Went   85
The Victor   86
Lines for Jack Clemo   86
The Wastrel   87
Keys   88
The Summerhouse   89
The Tale-Teller   90
Another Country   91
'It cannot come because desired'   92
A Marriage   93
'Who was it came'   94
Another Border   95

From *Broken Laws* (1970)

Aphrodite   99
A Fortune   100
Over the rim   101
In the Graeco-Roman Room   102
A Trip   103
A Special Train   104
A Natural Philosopher   105
A Historian   106
A Dreamer   107
A Marked Man   108
A Casualty   109
A Waking   110
Resolution   110
Northern Lights   111
Snow   111
February   111
Thaw   112
An April   112
Summer Solstice   112

Contents   ix

Singing   113
The Sounds   113
This Silence   114
I am the Sun   114
Aubade   115
Snatches for Charles Ives   115

From *The Center of Attention* (1974)

After God   119
The Twentieth Century   121
Dark of the Moon   122
The Center of Attention   123
The Translators' Party   126
The Princess Casamassima   128
Power   130
The Sonnet   131
Print-Out Song   132
O Personages   133
Comanches   134
Brainwaves   135
Tree   136
Shrew   137
Boar   138
Dogfish   139
Blood   140
Egg   141
Rats   142
Eagles   144
Burning Bush   145
Shell   145
Wherever   146
The Wanderer   147
Runner   148
Sickness   149
Evening   149
A Dread   150

A Woe   150
Thought I Was Dying   151
Vows   152

Hang-Gliding from Helicon

I

Himself   158
His Steps   159
A Stone   159
Folk Tale   160
The Sacred Fount   161
Possession   161
Stop the Deathwish! Stop It! Stop!   162

II

The Great American Novel   164
Asleep   165
A Barn Burnt in Ohio   166
High Society   167
At the Roman Wall, 1956   170
Fontaine-les-Dijon Revisited   172
Reasons   173
Night Fishing   174
Ode to Joy   175

III

The Battle of Hastings   178
Witnesses   180
Jogger   183
Crack!   184
Slick   185
Mother   186
Scrolls from the Dead   186
Halflives   187
The Finish   188

IV

David's Folly   192
Great Owl   192
A Stillness   193
That Morning   194
Old Reprobate   195
Last Lynx   197
At Don's Garage   198
Ants   200
Lines for Scott Nearing   201
A Felled Tree   202

V

Words   204
Problems of Knowledge   206
Essay on Style   207
Crossing Walt Whitman Bridge   210
Mark Twain, 1909   213
A Letter to W. H. Auden   214
Her Obedient Servant   216
Reflections   217

Hang-Gliding from Helicon

The Poem

Arriving at last,

It has stumbled across the harsh
Stones, the black marshes.

True to itself, by what craft
And strength it has, it has come
As a sole survivor returns

From the steep pass.
Carved on memory's staff
The legend is nearly decipherable.
It has lived up to its vows

If it endures
The journey through the dark places
To bear witness,
Casting its message
In a sort of singing.

From
An Armada of Thirty Whales (1954)

Incubus

What did the caterpillars do
last time the Phoenix died?
    They beat their breasts with a hundred fists
till one of them espied
the egg the ashes incubate.
Then, sure that wings would flame again,
they broke their bread on a mulberry leaf
and out of himself each wove the sheath
from which he'll burst on flaming wings
    after the peace of a season's sleep,
    after the peace of a season's sleep.

What did the little children do
when Christ was last time crucified?
    Each hid beneath a mulberry wreath
and on one another spied.
For they were playing Prisoner's Base
and as the teams hid face to face
the only thing that mattered much
was which was caught and which would catch
    before the evening grew more dark,
    before the earth and air grew dark.

The seals in Penobscot Bay

hadn't heard of the atom bomb,
so I shouted a warning to them.

Our destroyer (on trial run) slid by
the rocks where they gamboled and played;

they must have misunderstood,
or perhaps not one of them heard

me over the engines and tides.
As I watched them over our wake

I saw their sleek skins in the sun
ripple, light-flecked, on the rock,

plunge, bubbling, into the brine,
and couple & laugh in the troughs

between the waves' whitecaps and froth.
Then the males clambered clumsily up

and lustily crowed like seacocks,
sure that their prowess held thrall

all the sharks, other seals, and seagulls.
And daintily flipped the females,

seawenches with musical tails;
each looked at the Atlantic as

though it were her looking-glass.
If my warning had ever been heard

it was sound none would now ever heed.
And I, while I watched those far seals,

tasted honey that buzzed in my ears
and saw, out to windward, the sails

of an obsolete ship with banked oars
that swept like two combs through the spray

And I wished for a vacuum of wax
to ward away all those strange sounds,

yet I envied the sweet agony
of him who was tied to the mast,

when the boom, when the boom, when the boom
of guns punched dark holes in the sky.

An armada of thirty whales

(Galleons in sea-pomp) sails
over the emerald ocean.

The ceremonial motion
of their ponderous race is

given dandiacal graces
in the ballet of their geysers.

Eyes deep-set in whalebone vizors
have found a Floridian beach;

they leave their green world to fish.
Like the Pliocene midge, they declare

their element henceforth air.
What land they walk upon

becomes their Holy Land;
when these pilgrims have all found tongue

how their canticles shall be sung!
They nudge the beach with their noses,

eager for hedgerows and roses;
they raise their great snouts from the sea

and exulting gigantically
each trumpets a sousaphone wheeze

and stretches his finfitted knees.
But they who won't swim and can't stand

lie mired in mud and in sand,
And the sea and the wind and the worms

will contest the last will of the Sperms.

At Provincetown

Over the wharves at Provincetown
we watched the hooded gulls manoeuvre.

As one last gull, in late arrival,
flung his wings before our face

crying *'Wait!,'* . . . *'Wait!,'* in a race
to ride their aerial carousel,

we saw his dark-dipt head, eye-bead,
each individual grace recede

as all swooped up, then spun, and fell
unmoving in motion. Here was pure flight,
free from all bird-appetite.

Then the highest soarer saw
the *Mary Magdalena* yaw
laden low with mackerel.

*   *   *

Beauty is the moment moving
toward unpremeditate perfection.

Over the wharves at Provincetown
the gulls within our arteries soaring

almost complete the great mobile
that all but froze gullsblood to steel.

Other wings across the harbor
flash like swords and dive for garbage.

That the pear delights me now

    That the pear's boughs
delight me now is
inconsequential.

But after fragrance come
bull bumblebees.
On ozone wings they hum,

on hairyhorny knees
rudely they enter,
nuzzle, gnash, & guzzle

nectar of the pear.
Roystering honeymakers,
wholly unaware

of the dust their bristles brought,
of the lovestrong draught
they pour down those pear-pistils.

    It's June now, and the petals
have dropped, dried, crumbled,
in dust they've blown away.

Bees snarl in thick thistles;
pearboughs, hung in the hot day,
sprout green nubs now. Birdcalls

drench the leaves like fragrance;
fruit grows opulent in
summer lightning, heat, rains.

Sensuous the pears hang
richly, sweet and bursting.
Pears plop down. Birds follow, thirsting.

    Nights nip the earthskin tighter,
sap stops of a morning,
sunred leaves more harshly flutter;

old pears the starling pecked at
wrinkle in the waning shade.
Fruit sourly lies, rejected

till it's out of the earth invaded:
maggots rapaciously & noiseless
fatten on fermented juices

and the gristle wriggles through
their sniggling tails & slime
spreads beneath the peartree.

 Some squush remains, though,
some meat around the seed.
When Indian Summer strains

the last warmth through the orchard
pearpits feast and feed
and stir, & burst, & breed:

Earthward plunge the tendrils.
 That the pear delighted me
is wholly incidental,

for the flower was for the fruit,
the fruit is for the seed.

The clams

     In the Bay of Fundy the clams
lie stranded, half-dry, by the tides

forty feet higher than sea
in killdeer's kingdom.

     Underground, they erect valved snouts.
Wet freckles sprout over the beach:

Each trickles a droplet, and each
attests to the desperate hope

that attends each ritual drop.
     Lie ten-hours-buried in sand

and the swirl of salt and the wet
seems an Age before suffering began.

All shrinks in the rage of the sun
     save the courage of clams, and their faith:

Sacrificing the water they breathe
seems to urge the tall moon from her orbit;

she tugs ocean, cubit by cubit
over killdeer's kingdom

and ends parched freedom.
     Moon, with sky-arching shell

and bright snout nine thousand miles long
and anemones in her kelp hair

that gleam in the heaven around her,
     responds with the wave of their prayers

or sucks the sea unawares.

Old Bug up there

On Faneuil Hall there squats a copper
more-than-man-sized green grasshopper.

Impaled above the Farmers' Market,
snow-slow smoke and sleet have darkened

him. His mandibles munch the seedless wind.
No hunger's his, no brass caresses;

he leaps the rooftops toward no granary.
Lashed by acerb winds he spins

to point the way. But men are heedless.
    Old Bug, you remind me of someone,

like you above a city raised
to seem far larger than alive.

You're not the only one that's placed
on such an eminence. And if

fewer follow your globe-eyed gaze now
than when this harbor was spined with masts,

I'll tell you bluntly, you're not first
nor last to point out true unfollowed ways.

On the extinction of a species

Avast, the Pileated Woodpecker:
Square-hole-knocker in the pine,
Wears his ivory tower as hatchetnose
Crested with a wedge of flame,
& busily bangs his wooden signature.

Death drops more birds than birds drop eggs
—Promethean feathers on suburban hills
Are rare. But those square holes
[Dark images] in a living frame
Endure , endure , endure , endure .

The larks

An exaltation of larks arising
With elocutionary tongue
Embellish sound on morning air
Already fringed with scent of dung;
The curate in his curacy
Hearkens to that natural song,
And maids like wood-doves in their purity
Rise to matins' golden dong.
Their prayers are sweet high exultations
Whereon untrammelled spirits wend,
Forgetting flesh and breakfast. Under
The rectory eaves, the larks descend.

The voice of the woodthrush, played at half speed,

reveals to the halting ear
the fullstopt organ that pours through floodgate reed
such somersaults of sound like waters falling
in dark crystal chambers
on iron timbrels

withholds from what we hear
those haunting basses, loud but too deepkeyed.
This slow bisected bird's yet wilder calling
resounds on inward anvil:
pain is mortal, mortal.

Auricle's oracle

Intensity, when greatest, may
Prove ludicrously small.
Who concentrates compellingly
More than the snoutish snail,
Hauling gunless turret up
Perpendicular glass,
    By muscle of mind and bodily ooze advancing,
    Atop at last the aquarium glass balancing?

Yet passion at its most intense
Consumes the minuscule.
The focus of the spirit's lens
On whatever the self may will
Like sunlight squeezed through a reading-glass
Turns trash to flame. The ooze congeals
    In a golden signature of snail-identity,
    Etched in glass by the snail's and the sun's intensity.

Ephemeridae

    Dark specks whirr like lint alive in the sunlight.
The sky above the birches is disturbed.

Swarms swarm between pure heaven and treetops:
it's the mayflies' four-hour frenzy before their fall.

Waterward, they lay eggs in their dying
spasms, having then endured it all.

    For five long shimmering afternoons that summer
we walked beneath the birchgroves on the shore

and watched the empty light on leaftips pour
and out of nowhere whirled the nebulae,

gadding gilded, all green energy, toward death.
    After, the birches stirred, and we beneath

saw south-flying mallards bleak the air.
Green turns husk now. The world's shrunk to the bone.

    Our thin flesh alone
through this long, cold, fruitless season

scampers frantic in wild whirligig motion
while larvae of the mayfly wait

and mallards migrate and the sap runs slow;
ours alone from time strains to purchase

    pleasures mayflies find among the birches.

I dreamt my love a-dying lay

while I beside her stood austere
to see my paradise decay;
From underneath the ground I heard
her tunnelled agony of despair
ricochet from earth to air;
I learned the word that Adam's ear
in Eden heard the day Man fell
(Who, tasting Mercy, swallowed Hell).
And then I saw Death lovingly
take his long fingers from the scythe
to gather ants & worms & me
from out the muck wherein we writhed.
He laid me where my coffin sits
and nailed the lid with cigarettes.
He wove a lily garland sweet
which insects crawled upon to eat.
Then he laid my coffin down
in the lonesome graveyard ground.
Down he laid my coffin, by
the bed wherein my savior died.

From
A Little Geste (1960)

In the Beginning

On the jetty, our fingers shading
incandescent sky and sea,

my daughter stands with me.
'Boat! Boat!' she cries, her voice

in the current of speech cascading
with recognition's joys.

'Boat!' she cries; in spindrift
bobbling sails diminish,

but Kate's a joyous spendthrift
of her language's resources.

Her ecstasy's contagion
touches the whirling gulls

and turns their gibbering calls
to 'Boat! Boat!' Her passion

to name the nameless pulls her
from the syllabic sea.

She points beyond the jetty
where the uncontested sun

wimples the wakeless water
and cries, 'Boat!' though there is none.

But that makes no difference to Katy,
atingle with vision and word;

and why do I doubt that the harbor,
in the inner design of truth,

is speckled with tops'ls and spinnakers,
creased with the hulls of sloops?

Kate's word names the vision
that's hers; I try to share.

That verbal imagination
I've envied, and long wished for:

the world without description
is vast and wild as death;

the word the tongue has spoken
creates the world and truth.

Child, magician, poet
by incantation rule;

their frenzy's spell unbroken
defines the topgallant soul.

The Hermit of Cape Rosier

    The hermit of Cape Rosier has three houses:
One's atop the cragged bluff that leaps
splashing spruce out of the water, hackled pines
sawing a jagged hole in heaven.   There
the hermit's house is: no door, windows like wounds,
a ribcage in a hat whose brim is eaves.
You have to know the path up there to find it;
even if you know the old back trail
you have to know the cut-off to the hermit's,
and when you get there, through the thorned blackberries
with the arched gulls shrill in the steep wind
you see   Keep Out   No Trespassing   assigned
on trees and staves.   Perhaps you are not welcome.
'Hello! Hello!' The winds snatch 'Lo!' and dash it
cragward, crumpled, down.   A seahawk's nest
in winter, filled with lichen and picked fishbones
would be as hospitable as is this homestead.
Why would anyone not born to feathers
seek such isolation in the sun?
All that the senses touch up here is cleanly,
scoured by solitude in the harsh height.
Yet grant a hermit reasonable cause
to abjure our fendered comforts, still one might
search his self for the natural parts of man
in scenes more clement.   Not the bleak of air
but ripeness of the earth, in summertime:
sometimes, beneath the blackberries, he searches there.

    The second house the hermit lives in
some people wouldn't call a house, unless
sleeping in a cave's compatible
with the human lot.   No one at Harborside
knows what got into Jethro
crouching like a woodchuck in his tunnel
while a scourge of moles rips furrows his father turned.
He's got good lands back there he never touches
except a potato plot and a row of beans;
nobody knows why Jethro won't be seen
at Meeting, store, or trade; nobody knows
just how he lives there, holed up like a marmot

while rains fall, and hay rises, and teams
move from field to field in hot July.
In woods, in the dead of summer, there's the smell
of green gone sour, of flesh the owl has killed;
delicate leafmould works its webbed decay,
a footstep stirs the leaves, and simmering death
bursts from earth behind a canopy
of green hands, giddy in the wind, that grasp the sun.
The cool of cave-mouth in the hill is dank,
the spindling spider hangs numb from his wheel,
the hemlock-guarded air is cold and still.

    The other house the hermit lives in
was once a boathouse, but he has no boat.
You pass clam baskets, broken, pyramided,
and mattocks worn down at the shiny tines,
split oars, stacked driftwood, a pile or two of shells.
Peering through the fogstained saltpocked window
imagine Jethro fingering his trove:
great conches curling empty till his ear brings
titanic surfs to tunnels the silent snail
polished in solitude; bright rocks whose stain
of emerald or quartz shaft of shine the starfish
hugged beneath the tide.

    Death seems nearer Jethro than it may be,
though in the village they say he's hale and sound.
Life seems precarious on his hillside,
battering windy breakers, by rot deepgnawed,
uncivil, ashake with joy and awe and wonder
at cragged Borealis
and the empty shell left on the shore.

Exploration

I am who the trail took,
nose of whom I followed,
woodwit I confided in
through thorned-and-briared hallows;
favoring my right side for
clouds the sun had hemmed in.
Behind the North I sought daystar,
bore down highroads hidden
to undiscerning gaze.
My right, my right I turned to
on trails strangely unblazoned
where fistfive forkings burgeoned,
I took my right. Was destined,
among deerdroppings on the ridge
or chipmunk stones astrain
or hoofmucks in the swampcabbage
to err? Landmarking birch
selfmultiplied in malice till
woods reared a whitebarred cage
around my spinning eye. The spool
of memory had run out my yarn
and lost the last hank. Found
I the maze I wander in
where my right, trusted hand,
leads round and round a certain copse,
a sudden mound of stone,
an anthill humming in the rocks
an expectant tune?
Lacklearning now my knowledge is
of how to coax recalcitrant
ignition from cold engines,
or mate a fugue in either hand
on spinet or converse
in any tongue but stonecrop signs.
Clouds hump like battling bulls. The firs
lash me with angry tines,
shred my clothes. A windwhipped will
uncompassed, lacking fur or fang,
strange to these parts, yet whom the anthill
anticipating, sang.

Safari

You need an empty burlap
bag; rubber boots;
a forked longhandled stick.
You need nerves like roots

of the willow half underwater
that stiffen the trunk they grip
though that trunk holds boughs aquiver
at the quietest breath.

You kneel on the willow's knees
probing the fern-rimmed ditch
till an arrow furrows the water,
till quiet is cleft by hiss

and quick and true the sinew
tightens in your arm, in your throat
and true and quick the long stick
lunges: a thunderbolt

pinions the diamond head
where the forking tongue is set
immobilizing nothing
else of that undulant jet —

I see those brave safaris
and my triumphal returns,
the writhing bag that dangles
from the forked stick's horns,

that dangles over the rosebuds
staked to the trellis I passed,
home through the tended garden
my prize held fast

— 'To do *what* with those creatures?
You'll drown them in the drain at once!' — and dream
of a boy, rigid, goggling
down the manhole's gloom

at serpents hugely striding
in the diamonded darkness agleam
and thrashing the still black waters
till they foam and rise like cream.

Flushing Meadows, 1939

Lightning! Lightning! Lightning! Without thunder!
A zaggedy white trombone of lightshot, crackling
Between metallic globules, egglike, hugely
Aching in the corners of our eyes —
The afterburn of electrocuted air
Sizzled into our ears and nostrils, halfblinded
Us. We reeled into the dim sunshine
Groping a little, holding hands, still hearing
The confident vibrant voice of the sound system —
'Harnessed . . . power . . . unnumbered benefits . . .'
And this we pondered down the bedecked Concourse
Of Nations. A gold-robed King of Poland brandished
Crossed swords on horseback pedestalled on high;
The Soviet Citizen bore his sanguine star
Almost as high as that American flag
That snaffled in the smart wind perched atop
The Amusement Park's live parachute drop.
Trapped in antique mores, now the sun
Abandoned the International Pavilions
To miracles of manmade light. The trees
In their pots were underlit, revealing pasty
Backsides of their embarrassed leaves. We barked
The shins of our puppylove against the crowds
That swirled around us, swirled like fallen leaves
In the wind's vortex toward the Pool of Fountains:
Mauve and yellowing geysers surged and fell
As national anthems tolled, amity-wise,
From the State of Florida's Spanish Carillon.
What portent, in that luminous night to share
Undyingly, discovery of each other!
Helen, Helen, thy beauty is to me
Like those immutable emblems, huge and pure —
One glimmering globe the world's will unifying
Beside spired hope that ravels the deep skies,
Our time's unnumbered benefits descrying
In their own light's shimmer, though the new dawn comes
With lightning, lightening in a murmur of summer thunder.

In the Days of Rin-Tin-Tin

In the days of Rin-Tin-Tin
There was no such thing as sin,
No boymade mischief worth God's wrath
And the good dog dogged the badman's path.

In the nights, the deliquescent horn of Bix
Gave presentiments of the pleasures of sex;
In the Ostrich Walk we walked by twos—
Ja-da, jing-jing, what could we lose?

The Elders mastered The Market, Mah-jongg,
Readily admitted the Victorians wrong,
While Caligari hobbled with his stick and his ghoul
And overtook the Little Fellow on his way to school.

Awoke into a Dream of Singing

Awoke into a dream of singing.
Birds amassed their gloried peals,
Drenching the deadwood with their ringing.
I could not breathe that air, all song.

Those trees, studded with autumn's plumage,
Bore no leaves that made no sound.
The fountain at their knees cascaded
Icicles. From brazen wound

The statue gushed. That air, so chill
With reedy-beaked insistent song,
Clotted fountain's-blood to crystal.
I could not breathe that air, all song.

From
The City of Satisfactions (1963)

A New Birth

While I turned in a warm cocoon
Man and Rome fell.
Furrows scarred the valleys.
Haggle, blow and toil
Echoed at the stony gates,
Yet discipleship to the seasons
Made gay the festival.

All that long labor made me
Who split my earthling skin
In a fallen wind, a dusty sky.
What patrimony I come by
Lies, an empty sack,
Shrivelled fables at my back.
This is a new birth I begin.

A Meeting

He had awaited me,
The jackal-headed.

He from Alexandria
In the days of the Dynasts,

I from Philadelphia
In a time of indecisions.

His nose sniffed, impassive,
Dust of the aeons.

A sneeze wrenched my brain
—I couldn't control it.

His hairy ears listen
Long. He is patient.

I sift tunes from the winds
That blast my quick head.

His agate eye gazes
Straight ahead, straight ahead.

Mine watch clocks and turn
In especial toward one face.

I thank Priestess of Rā
Who brought us together,

Stone-cutters of Pharoah
And The Trustees of

The British Museum.
When with dog-eared Anubis

I must sail toward the sun
The glistering Phoenix

Will ride on our prow;
Behind the hound-voices

Of harrying geese
Sink the cities of striving,

The fiefdoms of change
With which we have done,

Grown in grandeur more strange,
More heroic than life was

Or the dark stream at peace,
Or wings singed in the sun.

The Chosen

I am the one that drew
The black cake from the fire.
Then the sun throbbed
With blood's accusations.

Skulking fox and ferret snarl
In the dry rocks
At my tread.
Trees lock their arms against me.

The buzzard whose hover
Over the living
Spreads dread
Stills the wind above me

Whatever the track I follow.
Stones speak:
I have no fellows.
What did I do among them,

When, till this day
My lusts were young
And I lived as they live,
Bruising the earth,

That was worse than their wrongs
Or deserving their worst
Who last night lived as I lived
And now fling me forth?

The Unchosen

I didn't feel good
Even when I
Drew a white one. My blood

Beat like the toll
Of a bell in a blizzard.
Still ashake with fear's dole,

I watched him stand
Right beside me, and smile,
The black cake in his hand.

Then my belfry of bone
Nearly cracked out of pity
And—it missed me by *one*—

Joy. A stark stroke
Silenced the sun.
We stood still, stunned.

Then he cried out and broke
From our ring,
Ran alone, ran alone,

Raced up the heath.
As the sun oozed and bled
His lengthening

Shadow made dread
Hackle our marrow.
He grew with our dread

Til he was a shadow,
The gobbet that looms
On nightmare heath,

Presentiment of death
Committing our dooms,
Guilty of life.

We breathed the one breath,
Then with the one
Lunge, the one yell

We picked up stones.
We flung stones at its head.
The sun boomed like a bell—

We returned together.
We roasted the meat together.
We drank, we rejoiced together.

We were safe. We felt good.

Climbing Katahdin

Hoisting yourself
From fingerniche to toehold,
Approaching the Knife-Edge,

A deep shagged ravine gapes on the one side,
The eye of a blueberry-silver pool steep
Down the dizzydrop other,

Your breath short,
Each rib rasping,
Grasping the thinned air above the timberline,

Clinging
To the desolate rocks
Below the snowline,

You can believe
As others have believed—
This stony ridgepole bracing

Heaven the longhouse of the mountain,
Ktaadn.
You breathe his breath.

Hoisting yourself
Atop the spined ridge you'll find
On a slight plateau

Stretching toward the peak's rise
Huckleberries growing
Beside a spring!—you laugh at the surprise

Of it and chew in the icy air
Bursting berries big as birds' eggs,
Your lips and tongue relish the purple—

Then arise from feasting
On silvery frosted fruit
In the desolation

To hoist yourself,
From fingergrip to toehold
Each breath grasping

As high up as the mountain allows you.

In That High House

In that high house half up a hill
A string linked your hand to my hand.
From the swollen sea that gnashed the shore
A road coiled round the hill's stone breast.
Our string pulls taut, frays, snaps apart.
The castle's ruined, a winter's tree.
You mustn't cry now, little son.
The rooftree's fallen and the moon
Through skeletal shadows lights the hall.
Beyond the broken door a road
Coils round the ridges of a hill
Where another house may stand
And your hand loop another hand
And when that filament frays and falls
In roofless walls remember us
When most together most alone.

Saint-Apollinaire

September sunlight,
apples in the baskets,
potatoes in the bins,
rabbits in the barn,
cordwood under the outside stairs,
a tile-topped chimney lisping woodsmoke
pungent in the evening air,
odor of apples seeping through the floorboards,
nightlong dried-earth smell of the potatoes,
furtive skitters in the darkness,
mousefeet in the bins,
mice along the rafters,
snug in the farmhouse,
live coals in the grate the whole night long.
Dew stiffens gelid grass leaves.
Steps crunch the pebbly path
bringing bread in the morning,
morning bread
to Saint-Apollinaire.
We push dark shutters outward.
Their rims dazzle in lightfalls pouring
over the windowsill in splashes
awash on the scrubbed tiles.
The children in their smocks are singing
their schoolward way among the asters.

Dijon

In November they pollarded the plane trees,
   bound the branches into besoms,
      stacked faggots
to dry through half the winter by the wall.

Our Katy cried to see those amputees
   bear wintry rime on clumps of stumps
      like veterans of wars,
undecorated files at crooked rest.

The empty sleeve-men, one on a leg of pole,
   hump their ways among the plane trees
      in crooked ranks
as Maquis infiltrate the guarded flanks

of courts, and vanish in a clank of gates
   to warm the marrow of their wounds
      at hissing hearths
where lopped branches redly singe and sigh.

When woodsmoke lifts from the Place de la République
   and air between the walls grows clearer
      the lined trees,
rainwashed familiars of paucity, remain,

Their knobs aswell with nodes of summer's verdure
   as though time and the sun could nurture
      and eke a future
of live limbs tousling the wind from every suture.

Vezelay

Preach me no preachments John Ruskin
of the Aspiration of pointed Arches,
of the 'wing'd nobility' of buttresses.
I have voyaged over waters for the laving of my sight.
I have found a still font
where in the amber twilight
from column to column the arches
leap, and the light hallows
the curvature of hollows
the rhythm of the columns
the anthems of the silence
ethereal masses. Heaven's
obsidian light pours down
on the joyous Doomsday
of Christ and the creatures
the zodiac of vintners
the sacrifice of oxen
the dogheaded devils
peoples of the earth.
Our sins upon the capitals
breathe in rippling light,
move in the fluent light,
move in their own commission
till in the mind this moment
turns stone,
stone in the mind carved
with devildogs and virgins
butchering the ox in
stone relief, the drunken
vintners in the mind's eye
stony-eyed, the creatures
of the mind arrested,
gargoyle imagination's
personae held in stone
carven on the capitals
under rippling vaultribs
dancing down the arches.
Each in the absolute
joy of strict proportion
leaps from stone to stone

image of the earthfolk,
image of this moment
carved in the mind,
all dooms dancing
toward that stone Resurrection:
Breath on the Tympanum.

1956

That week the fall was opulent. Vendanges,
> Dancing, sunlight, autumn warmth, full larder
> Before the endurable oncome of the winter.

Needing a haircut, I asked the coiffeur again
> To cut it short. He shrugged, but, being genial,
> Complied. A Samson came in for his marcel.

Musique à la radio cut short: Shrill voice:
> Our fleet en route to liberate Suez!
> Nasser, beware! Victory in two days!

Then glory used up all the largest type fonts
> As Napoleonic ghosts in parachutes
> Converged canalward on those camel-troops.

Coiffeur and Samson were ready for the glory.
> But Egyptians, seeing Israel's guns, skedaddled
> Before the Indo-China vets embattled

Them. The RAF pounded the desert
> For two days. Meanwhile John Foster Dulles
> (My countryman) put through long distance calls

To God again, and passed The Moral Law
> Again. Texas and Oklahoma cheered
> His oil on troubled waters. It appeared

OK to Moscow too. Peace took the UN
> By unsurprise. Beaten yet once again,
> Dienbienphu yet unavenged, Pétain

Yet unavenged, Verdun . . . My hair grew longer.
> I went to the coiffeur again. This day
> In short supply I found l'amitié.

I spoke of soccer, not Suez, nor glory.
> His shears yet jabbed my head most dangerously.
> The next man up read 'Combat' sullenly.

L'amitié is scarce. A run on soap.
> Hoarders have got the rice. There's no coal
> In the coalyards. At the school, no oil;

What's plenty? A pyramid in the Magasin
>   Of canned-for-America grapefruit, tin on tin;
>   A sign says: 'PAMPLEMOUSSES ISRAËLIENS.'

The ration of gas threatens the Cabinet.
>   Canal-boats on the Ouche fray weedy hausers.
>   Nobody mentions glory now, or the Gaza,

But curses the malign sphinx of history.
>   By the Arc de Triomphe they await who'll unriddle the past
>   And may, even now, be descending the mountain path.

A Letter to Wilbur Frohock

St-Apollinaire (Côte d'Or)
November, 1956

Cher Maître:

Neither my explication
of 'Le Dernier Abencérage'
nor the almost-fluency
at quip and badinage

attested by your A minus
a decade ago
in 'Oral Intermediate
French' suffices now;

a beret is not enough.
Je puis acheter du pain
mais, when I go to the coalyard
as I do, again and again,

my first word or gesture's
carte d'identité,
sufficient proclamation:
'JE SUIS ÉTRANGER.'

'Sell you coal? My poor mother
Burns faggots in her mountain hovel—
You've la bombe atomique in your country—
Our children go barefoot in winter'

la marchande rails, distrait—
Besides, her coalyard's bare;
but, as you've said, the structure
—impeccable—of their

grammar reflects the logic
of the French mind. We've been here
two months. By now the neighbors
say 'Bonjour, Monsieur';

in our village there are two eggs
for sale each second day,
reserved for the toothless aged
or a sick bébé

and when our boy got queasy
and couldn't take his meat
at l'épicerie they sold me
un oeuf for him to eat—

My accent's improving.

Gestures

Before train-time they swept across the track
Bare-headed or beretted, in a tide
    Bearing loaves
Of *pain d'épice*, bottles of Nuits-St-George
And Chambertin. The engine nudged a furrow
Across their crest and chuffled to a stop.
    They thrust the loaves and bottles

Of the best they had to give toward open windows
Where, bleared and grizzled, the late triumphant hosts
    Of Budapest
Outstretched their hands in pauperage and pain
And pride. *Vive la liberté! Vive
La liberté!* chanted the crowd. The few
    With French enough replied

'Merci' for Dijon's gifts of gratitude,
Of homage to their hopeless hope, of guilt
    That others died,
That others fought and fled, their future left
Behind, that boy propped on a hard-backed bench,
A swollen bullet in his throbbing arm,
    While we communed with *pain*

D'épice and *premiers crûs*. The engine, watered,
Whooshed and strained. The stock began to roll
    Toward the mountains:
A disused camp for Prisoners of War
Would roof them in while squat Red tanks patrol
All homeward roads past Austria. Then peace
    Settled from grimy skies

As a wild gull, daubed in coaltar, flounders
Disconsolately down to a joyless rock.
    In bitter weather
We heard that some escaped Hungarians,
One with a sling, from Dole toiled up the Juras
Toward the immaculate freedom of that zone
    That looms in Alpine snow.

Mi-Carême

We were surprised by Mi-Carême's obtruding
On half the acerb season, when the fishes'
Trials of frailty almost seemed habitual.
A small renunciation of the flesh is
A thorn, though not in truth a crown, until
What's done without no longer pricks regret.
Well, on the rue de la Liberté that day
The breeches' bulge, the gaygrin becks all told
In winks of mask what fireworks stuttered out:
The frivolous feast has come, beneath the gaze
Of Jacquemaire, who, steeple-tall, emerged
At the booming sennet of his hourly bells.
Such images as these helped to dispel
Almost all trace of Lenten abnegation
In resurrections of the corpse interred
At Mardi Gras:
                Those monsters at Chalon
Had made incomparable mirth. Some strode
On longlegs teetering past the crowded eaves;
A pair of osier giants, heads like eggs
The last roc laid before the earth grew cool,
In couthless courtship dipped and ducked and danced,
Joy's colossi, rathe for ridicule,
Tunes tattered the air festooned with flags then
As instrumental joculators wove
In sinuous undulations in between
His lumbering ankles and the porte-cochère
That a nest of pulleys held in her skirts aloft.
Now green snow fell, turned paper in our hair
As La Reine des Roses in her sheen negligée
Floated on a swan afloat on streams
Of streamers, bobbing heads and foams of sound.
Then fezzed trombonist, houri tambourine,
Libidinous flügelhorn and urgent drum
Conducted onward all these orotund
And liberal-featured figments of our glee
Beyond the turret-portals of the city
With peals of jubilation, casting them
To exile in a wilderness of marshes.
On tabletops, from our café, we leaned toward

Their unabated pantomime, their sway
To inaudible rhythms as the wind returned
An intermittent summons from the river.
There, across the high bridge to the island
A grave tribunal of the bishopric
Attended, palled in funeral pomp, and poised
To cinder all that gaiety in the end.

At Mi-Carême they dance before me still,
Made midget by the distance, silhouettes
Moving mirrored over the sheen of Saône,
Their procreant gestures ravelling sky and water
With earth till purification of the flame.
Now false-faced gamins shake their clipper-clappers
Against the Lenten rectitude, remembering
The boil of blood, the surge of seed, the sensual
Plentitude before the human legend
Recalls us to supernal imitation
And the weights of sorrow under the haloed sun.

The Pursued

Surely he'd outwitted them, outdistanced them and earned
Respite at this café. There goes the ferry.
Two trips risked in his own person, over
And back, and now, in this wig
Crossed again. Nobody knew him.
Coffee under the arbor, mission done,
Content. And then he recognized
The first signs—
Heat, hotter than the day's heat, swarming
And his skin parched, stretching
Tight about each finger; the eyes
Pounding: arbor, harbor,
Table, gable, all begin to swing
Up and forth, forth and up, up and so, until
Giddily earth grinds beneath him, shudders;
Sweat oozes icy on his neck now,
On shaking chest a shirt of seaweed crawls,
Iron table rat-tat-tat-tat-tats against his elbow
Though harbor's calm and arbor's still. You've seen
A stepped-on centipede left on the pavement,
Each limb's oracular gesticulations?
—Cutting through the scent of pear trees
Klaxons, baying, toil up up the highroad,
Vans of his other pursuers.

The City of Satisfactions

As I was travelling toward the city of satisfactions
On my employment, seeking the treasure of pleasure,
Laved in the superdome observation car by Muzak
Soothed by the cool conditioned and reconditioned air,
Sealed in from the smell of the heat and the spines
Of the sere mesquite and the seared windblast of the sand,
It was conjunction of a want of juicy fruit
And the train's slowdown and stopping at a depot
Not listed on the schedule, unnamed by platform sign,
That made me step down on the siding
With some change in hand. The newsstand, on inspection,
Proved a shed of greyed boards shading
A litter of stale rags.
Turning back, I blanched at the Silent Streak: a wink
Of the sun's reflection caught its rear-view window
Far down the desert track. I grabbed the crossbar
And the handcar clattered. Up and down
It pumped so fast I hardly could grab hold it,
His regal head held proud despite the bending
Knees, back-knees, back-knees, back-knees propelling.
His eyes bulged beadier than a desert toad's eyes.
His huge hands shrank upon the handlebar,
His mighty shoulders shrivelled and his skin grew
Wrinkled while I watched the while we reeled
Over the mesquite till the train grew larger
And pumping knees, back-knees, we stood still and
Down on us the train bore,
The furious tipping of the levers unabated
Wrenched my sweating eyes and aching armpits,
He leapt on long webbed feet into the drainage
Dryditch and the car swung longside on a siding
Slowing down beside the Pullman diner
Where the napkined waiter held a tray of glasses.
The gamehen steamed crisp-crust behind the glass.
I let go of the tricycle and pulled my askew necktie,
Pushed through the diner door, a disused streetcar,
A Danish half devoured by flies beneath specked glass,
Dirty cups on the counter,
A menu, torn, too coffeestained for choices, told
In a map of rings my cryptic eyes unspelled

Of something worth the digging for right near by
Here just out beyond the two-door shed.
The tracks were gone now but I found a shovel,
Made one, that is, from a rusting oildrum cover,
A scrap of baling wire, a broken crutch,
And down I heaved on the giving earth and rockshards
And a frog drygasped once from a distant gulley
And up I spewed the debris in a range
Of peaks I sank beneath and sweated under till
One lunge sounded the clunk of iron on brass
And furious scratch and pawing of the dryrock
Uncovered the graven chest and the pile of earth downslid
While under a lowering sky, sweatwet, I grasped and wrestled
The huge chest, lunged and jerked and fought it upward
Till it toppled sideways on the sand. I smashed it
Open, and it held a barred box. My nails broke
On the bars that wouldn't open. I smashed it
Open and it held a locked box. I ripped my knuckles
But couldn't wrest that lock off till I smashed it
Open and it held a small box worked
In delicate filigree of silver with
A cunning keyhole. But there was no key.
I pried it, ripped my fingers underneath it
But couldn't get it open till I smashed it
Open and it held a little casket
Sealed tight with twisted wires or vines of shining
Thread. I bit and tugged and twisted, cracked my teeth
But couldn't loose the knot. I smashed it
Open and the top came off, revealing
A tiny casket made of jade. It had
No top, no seam, no turnkey. Thimblesmall
It winked unmoving near the skinbreak
Where steakjuice pulsed and oozed. I thought aroma
Sifted, thinning till the dark horizon
Seemed, and then no longer seemed, a trifle
Sweetened. I knelt before
A piece of desert stone. When I have fitted
That stone into its casket, and replaced
The lid and set that casket in its box,
Fitted the broken top and set that box within
The box it came in and bent back the bars
And put it in the chest, the chest back in the hole,

The peaks around the pit-edge piled back in the pit,
Replaced the baling wire and crutch and oildrum cover
And pushed back through the diner, will the train
Sealed in from the smell of heat and mesquite
Envelop me in Muzak while it swooshes
Past bleak sidings such as I wait on
Nonstop toward the city of satisfactions roaring?
If I could only make this broken top
Fit snug back on this casket

The Great Horse Strode Without a Rider

      The great horse strode without a rider.
He looked as though no bit had ever reigned him,
No girthstrap squeezed the gloss of his firm belly.
The glass store windows mirrored him in broken
Images he smartly paced between.
His hooves precisely clapt upon the pavement.
Pistol-shots sound like his taut tattoo.
Pedestrians in ant-swarms elbowed doorways
Crouched beneath his image in the glass
On Commerce Avenue, until he came
To where it broadens under aisles of trees.
Now he was trotting and the trees dropped shadows
Flicking on and off his flanks in ripples.
His jaunty nostrils gathered all the wind in
That strained through sweetened lindens. Now he breathed
An easy laboring while criss-crossing feet
Rapped sharp *accelerandos*. In the houses
Watchers dropped their gaze from square glazed cages
To caress his rump. Then he was gone,
Past the furthest gatehouse by the roadside
Where roadsides run to thistles in the daisies,
And I though not astride him yet beside him
Moving with like movement to his speed
Now watch him break into a frolic canter.
His capers kick the clods up leaping after.
Now breasting upward toward the wind he gallops.
His mane whips like the backlash of sea-breakers
Over the ridge while I'm still struggling upward
Over the ridge. He's running down the headland.
He's far beyond me now and yet I see him
In clarity beyond the meed of sight.
His mighty movements pull me as the moon
Toward the vast intensity of heaven
Tugs the laggard tides. He's poised there, leaping
To for an instant hang as the hawk hangs, plunge then
Forefeet stretched to part the weedy froth
And disappear below the hill's rock brow.
Laboriously I clambered down the cliffside,
Pushed my way through wave-smashed bluffs past tide-pools,
Came at last to the broken stone declivity

Where spittled breakers, foam on rippled chests
And heads wind-tossed in their relentless oncome,
Lunged out of the sea to heave before me
The hugeness of their purpose, on, and on,
In charge on echoing charge against the shore.

As I Was Going to Saint-Ives

As I was going to Saint-Ives
In stormy, windy, sunny weather
I met a man with seven wives
(The herons stand in the swift water).

One drinks her beer out of his can
In stormy, windy, and bright weather,
And who laughs more, she or her man?
(The herons stand still on the water.)

One knows the room his candle lit
In stormy, lightning, cloudburst weather,
That glows again at the thought of it
(Two herons still the swift water).

His jealous, wild-tongued, Wednesday's wife—
In dreepy, wintry, wind-lashed weather
—What's better than that ranting strife?
(Two herons still the roaring water.)

There's one whose mind's so like his mind
In streaming wind or balmy weather
All joy, all wisdom seem one kind
(The herons stand in the swift water).

And one whose secret mazes he
In moon-swept, in torrential weather
Ransacks, and cannot find the key
(Two herons stand in the white water).

He'll think of none save one's slim thighs
In heat and sleet and windy weather
Till death has plucked his dreaming eyes
(Two herons guard the streaming water).

And the one whose love moves all he's done,
In windy, warm, and wintry weather,
—What can he leave but speaks thereon?
(Two herons still the swift water.)

From
Striking the Stones (1968)

The Way It Is

They were waiting here to say
This is the way it is

This is the way

I came bawling into their domain
Of harsher light
Remembering a place
Of purer light and messages
Passed across a darkened transom
From that place
Remembering

They said this is the way it is
In this light this dust
This scuffle for the scraps, bad blood
Between unequals   You'll get wise
You can break
Your heart against stones here
Remembering.

Counsellors, betake your
Covenants of convenience
To a place of stones,

I
Must lift the shadow of each shadow
To find the dooryard
To that place.

There

Who'd go out there

On the black, humped
Slithering snarl of the sea

Past splintered
Rock hulls

Of islands wrecked by wave

Unless drawn
Inward

By her nets of song?

Testament

A bare tree holds the fog in place.

It seeps out of irregularities
In gnarled twigs, those crevices
A nuthatch has picked clean

—One time there was a hill
Behind this tree
Dropped down,

A prospect of the tumbling
Breakers curled.

Fog has grown out of a tree.
I am the only
Thing moving

In this country.
No sky
Over no hill
Above no curved horizon,

The world contracts,

Interchange of codicils
Between one stem of taut limbs
In the damp halflight

Of this birdless day
And another.

In the Pitch of Night

White-throat beyond my window,
The sliver of your song
Pierces
The mist before the morning light
Shrivels the promises of night.

Your song
Changes nothing. The cold bay
Heaves and settles as before.
I cannot see you
In your cloudy tree.

Why do you thrust your silver knife
Into my silences? What undelivered
Letter will you open
Slitting the folded edges
Of my sleep?

It is darker
Before my open eyelids
Than in the clarity before
When I was hearing
From a burning tree

A sparrow sing.
I could all but see him in the blaze.
His unappeasable desire
Threaded across the sky
A testament of change,

Melting into song
Those pure resonances only
That echo
Without cease
Through discords dying all the day.

In Provence

A sky too hot for photographs,
A sky that bakes the toplids of the eyes,
A withered olivetree
That scratches at the crotches of the clouds
And on the rock
Among the sockets of the shadows
Lizards stop, and dart—

Here, amid the airs
Sweetened, pierced by wild
Thyme in heat, wild lavender,
It is the same
As under austere cranes that hoist
A frame of walls
Between us and the rigid sky

—The eye daring
Insupportable light
To find those slits in the familiar
Through which we peer,
Glimpsing then,
Or here, the only
Changelessness we'll know.

*Instructions to a Medium, to be transmitted
to the shade of W. B. Yeats, the latter
having responded in a séance held on
13 June 1965, its hundredth birthday:*

You were wrong about the way it happens,
You, unwinding your long hank of that old yarn
    Spun from our common dream since chaos first receded,
    As though a superannuated Druid were needed.

What looms now on that desert where the birds
Turn in their frenzy and scream uncomprehending?
    Not a cradled beast in whom divinity
    Could repossess the earth with fierce majesty;

We've seen the coming of a dispensation
Miniaturized in our set on the tabletop:
    Blazing from its pad, that rigid rocket
    No larger than the ballpoint pencil in my pocket

With its sophisticated systems for manoeuvre
And retrieval, the bloated astronauts within
    Plugged to cardiometers in weightless flight
    —Their radiant spirals crease our outer night.

No, you were wrong about the way it happens.
Our radar scorns all horoscopes. Where Phaedrus
    Tumbling past perfection fell toward birth,
    Junked satellites in orbit ring the earth

And circuitry has made the Tetragrammaton
As obsolescent as a daft diviner's rod.
    Yet you, a boy, knelt under Knocknarea
    Where the cragged mountain buffeted the sea

And knew a cave beside that desolate shore
Had been the gate through which Christ harrowed Hell.
    But what could knowledge of that sort be worth?
    Imagination would not rest; from that day forth

God-driven, you toiled through our long-darkening age
To do the work the gods require. In love, in rage,
    You wrote no verse but glorifies the soul.
    What's history, that we should be imprisoned

By some contention of the passing minute,
No sooner won than lost by those who win it?
    All action's but a strut between the wings.
    Our part you knew we each must play by heart,

By heart-mysteries that no invention changes
Though knowledge further than our wisdom ranges.
    'What matter though numb nightmare ride on top?'
    You knew there'd be a perturbation in the skies,

You knew, whatever fearful turn would come
By our contrivance, or immortal from the womb,
    Violence must break old tables of the law
    And old solemnities toward desecration draw,

But how conceive coherence with our power?
Old ghost, you seem to beckon from your tower—
    Moon-magic is the grammar of your speech,
    A cast of thought to keep within our reach

The tragic gaiety of the hero's heart
That blazes where the soul consumes in art
    All reality as faggots for its fire,
    Revealing the desired in the desire.

Then man, though prisoned in his mortal day,
In imagination dominates all time,
    Creates that past and future between which his way
    Unwinds with the fated freedom of a rhyme.

Words for Dr. Williams

Wouldst thou grace this land with song?
    Well, go yodel your head off.
But if it's poems you want, then take a town
    with mills and chimneys, oil
Slithering on the river toward the falls,
    grit in the air, a man
Just off the night shift turning, tired yet strong
    to watch the girl who hurries
Toward a timeclock step down from the bus—
    slim ankles, one,
Two, and click click click swings past. The sun
    glints on her raincoat. There's
Your muse and hero. Stick around this town
    where people speak American
And love is possible—Your stethoscope
    held to our arteries
In sickness and in health you found some places
    where our own poems grow.

A Visitation

Now why would a visitation from the Isles
Of the Blessèd come to Sarthmore,
PA 19081, a borough zoned
For single-family occupancy? No
Rocks of Renunciation on our
Assessors' rolls. Somewhere,
A consecrated shore
Ringed by dolmens where the wind speaks.
I listen to the hunger of the owl
Enclose the chipmunk in the quavering night,
I hear the plantain stretch its leaves to smother
Grass-shoots reaching toward the light.
The thick obituary of a lost day
Lies still on our writhing lawn.
And now the sky, black widow, pales
At the arrival of her new lover.
Between the thighs of trees old graves of sorrows
Open, and a fresh wind stirs.

On the Industrial Highway

Approaching the Walt
Whitman Bridge you pass
an affluent world—

a subculture of spouts,
nozzles, ducts, a host
of snakes and ladders

in nests and thickets
or by tribes, laying
dinosaur farts

against the sun.
I drive slowly through the
stink and gawk at

shapes that no
familiarity breeds,
a ghostless city

called 'gas works,' never
meant for death or living.
A pipe pulses

flame in secret
code on the gashed sky.
Here are things

whose archetypes
have not yet been dreamed.
There's no more perfect

duct than these
ducts, pipes, facts
burdened with nothing

anticipating
unhappened memories,
visionary things.

Shaking the President's Hand

Who'd be likely to forget
His brief squeeze by those brisk fingers,
The First Citizen's! The touch of kings
Was blessed, a gift to remedy
The King's Evil. Here
Where every man's a king,
What did I touch a President to cure?

Crop-Dusting

The mice rot in their tunnels in a field
Where phantom harvesters cut phantom grain.
A poisoned acre grows a poisoned yield.

Here skinny children stretch their hands in vain.
Their swollen bellies hurt, and are not healed.
A phantom blade has harvested their grain.

Night after night I see this land annealed
By draughts of fire and death that fall like rain.
One poisoned acre poisons all the field.

These are my crops. We harrow my domain.
The one who pays counts all for which he's billed.
A phantom harvester stacks phantom grain.

To own such wealth as this my heart I've steeled
And all but stilled the tumult in my brain.
My poisoned acre grows a poisoned yield.

Unable to be dispossessed by Cain,
In his accounts my civil tithes are sealed.
And how renounce the poisoning of this field,
Or be forgiven the reaping of its grain?

The Peaceable Kingdom

[The Phi Beta Kappa Poem
Swarthmore College, 1964]

I

Now that we sponsor the extirpation of folklore,
    The growing scarcity of trees,
Bulldozers gouging roadbeds through the valleys,
    Traffic clogged where streams once flowed,
More people nourished by more Inplant Feeding,
    The disuse of Deer Crossing signs,
Proliferation of home-heliports,
    Attrition of the harvest-home
And slagheaps overshadowing the city,
    The mountain's heart quarried away,
Ingurgitation of knowledge by computers
    Whose feedback gives for wisdom facts
Elicited by robots or commuters
    Grown unhandy with real things
From much manipulation of abstractions,
    The seasons seldom touching them,
Not even benign falls of snow disguising
    A land it will be harder to love;

Where Opulence, demotic *arriviste*,
    Counts his costly toys like beads
While Penury gnaws knuckled fists, her brawling
    Brood of brats picking through trash,
The sullen disinherited and darker
    Faces massing in the square
As though impatient with their ill provision
    Despite the auspex of Dow Jones
That proves the National Gross Product growing,
    The deserts paved with fresh concrete,
Rumbling shadows of the freightcars tilting
    From mine to mill to guarded zone
And skies athrob with gaud and roar of firework,
    Gigantic needles jabbing high
Swiftly trailing flame like thread, then piercing
    The beady button of the moon,
Ashes on Wyoming's fodder falling,
    Milk curdled, stunted seed;

II

are we ready to go forth? Where you have come from
the students will be ever young; there it is only
the faculties and trees grow older. Leaving this friendly
hillside, you will reach your destinations—be sure
in your luggage, among trophies, clothes, and lists
of those Important Books as yet unread, to bring
the Catalogue of the Ships and tales of revolution
—the Russian, the Industrial—and explications
of both the valence table and the vertebrates
who, since the Good Duke dreamed a green world where the court
corrupts no man, agree upon hypotheses
that define the Good and tell the False from True.

III

Imperfect learning, bless this place
With possibilities of grace.
Let Mind, that ranges Heaven as far
As Barnard's pendant, lightless star,
Regard, though darkness shroud the soul,
Its constant living aureole
That casts one comprehending light
Across our chaos and the night;

Transform the deserts abstract thought
And unslaked selfishness have wrought
Into orchards where the trees
Stand rich with fruit, epitomes
Of sensuous joys that leap from birth,
Nourished in the dark of earth,
Toward sapling vigor crowned with flowers,
In acts as self-fulfilled as ours

Who build a city out of stone.
And in whose image is this done?
Defend our visionary quest,
Humane intelligence, that we
Who've eaten fruit from nature's tree
And know perfection but in art,
May, schooled and chastened by our past,
Conceive our city in the heart.

Open Letter, Returning a Questionnaire Unanswered

  —And blandish me not with the charisma
Of codex cards. I, a particular
One, a reveller irreducible in my
Republic of being, am sworn to resist
The unecstasy of the self's swift immolation
In your cold clasp of quantification.
Your multiple unchoice is irredeemable.
In none does any of my individual
Voices echo. To questions I wouldn't even ask
You mouth me answers I'd give not a syllable
Of acquiescence to. You come unbidden,
Passing beyond my identification number,
Age, sex, place of birth, to planted
Demands whose half-facts sprout five opinions
Only, excluding multiple truths. But opinions
Of half-facts are not the facts of opinion.
In the sleek city of your laws, where averages
Support constructions buttressed by totaled figures
I never come but in my ragged pocket
Carry a plot to silence the banquet speaker
And blast the foundation your fabrication stands on.
  No use to hide
In a blockhouse of filed statistics—there's no protection
In that steel box, excogitating card on card—
Well, I'm off again to my own land, scot-free,
Confiding my truths to the wind, but still on guard.

Breathing Purely

Now, at last,
I carry nothing
In my briefcase
And an empty mind.
In the meadow

Under the chestnut tree
I am a part of what I see.
Swallows above the alder thicket
Skim mosquitoes from the haze,
And I've seceded

From all committees, left
My Letters to the Editor unsent
No solutions, no opinions.
Breathing purely
Without ambitions, purged, awaiting

Annunciations of the true.
The wind is up now and the swallows gone.
I'll listen to the chestnut tree
Rustling
Empty-headed in the wind.

Banished

Tilting toward the hill with vacant frames
Webbed in windows, barn and springhouse fallen
Beneath one chestnut tree across a meadow
Gone to goldenrod and black-eyed susans—
So long unpeopled that nobody's name
Still clung like lichens to the rotting wood.
Home, this was, to a half-remembered story
Of desire denied, denied,
Of hope impossible and strange penance
Mutely lingering as the town grew round it.
Though times, though people changed, none quite forgot.
A house the wind blew through could still remind us,
A splintery house whose empty windows swung
With balls of light, aglow in summer darkness.
And if you took the steep path through the dooryard
After sledding on the far side of the hill,
Or trace of path cows may have once come down,
There'd come a sound unlike the crunch galoshes
Sink in snow with, or the runners' whoosh:
Two thumps, two thumps hard on a wooden floor,
Two thumps on wooden floor, heeltap, crutchtap
Eking a progress on a darkened stair
—Deep as your knees, snow-holes opened behind you
Till at the first lone streetlamp's civil glow
You dared to stop, shivering in brittle air,
Your hammer heart ashake—
                              But here are houses,
Tenanted—the hill's been levelled down
Till not a trace remains. The houses here now
Show bland walls of glass to one another,
Eaveless vistas. Here the glare of newness
Blinds to losses scarcely visible
Eyes above as yet unflowered beds
And shadeless shrubs in ranks of rawness.
Late model cars crouch paired in carport stalls—
Demesne of Unpast, happy subdivision,
All grieving injured ghosts are banished hence.
If through these picture windows shifting lights
Meander on the television screens
No fear need chill the neighbor children's marrow:
Nothing left abandoned here remains
Where all that is desired can be supplied.

Moving Among the Creatures

Moving among the creatures
As the new light
Surges down this cliff, these trees, this meadow,
Brightening the shade among the alders
And shrivelling the dew on leaves,
They are contented in their bodies—I can tell it—
The squalling gulls delighted to be turning
Widdershins, their shadows swooping
Over rocks where startled deer
Clatter, flashing spindly shanks
And delicate hooves while underfoot
Even the uglies in their sticky skins
Exult, the woodfrogs clunking all the bells
In sunken steeples, till at my
Thick tread
They leap and scissor-kick away
While the withering leech,
Shrinking, enlarging, waving
Knobbed horns
Makes the stem shine
With silver spittle where he's gone.
I trip on vines, stumble in potholes
And long for something of myself that's in them,
In the gulls' windy coursing, in the frogs'
Brief cadenza, even in the slug's
Gift to leave
A gleaming track, spun
From his own
Slippery gut.

Signatures

Wings outstretched, a horned owl
Nailed beneath a crown
Of antlers on the barn door

Shrivels in the wind,
And in the swale
Among black pellets,

Signatures of deer,
The wild roses of the field
—*Rosa Virginiana*—sway

As tall as trees. Each leafy bough
Beneath the deepest center of the sky
Is scented crimson as it's green with thorns.

There, on the sky's brim, floats
One lone jet too high
To break the day's long stillnesses.

Its white breath
Splits the sky.
The halves of heaven

Are bluer than each other.
All they cover leans to sign
Bequests of their significance,

Urgent as the center of the sun,
Yet silent
And invisible

As those fixed stars
We drift beneath
In the confusions of our light.

At Evening

At evening comes a certain hour
When the teeming world remembers
It is a hostage of the dead.

Then bend in homage
The tall trees whose sprinkle of seeds
Tickled the wind. The wind is dying.

This is the hour when dust
Gleams as the tired corona leans
Its bloodied head against the rim of sky

And the dark night girds
Beyond the pulsing stars
To drop its pomps of mourning down.

From windows of the houses come
Colloquial sounds and pungent odors,
Alien rhythms thrust against the night.

Far-Off Light

There are no constellations, only
Points of light
Daubed on the black slab of the night.

No gods in armor or reclining
Queens, no charismatic pizzles
On shining beasts. We do not find

Greek pictures
But trace our own creatures,
From dot to dot fill in our riddles

—Huge stallion plunges on the Milky Way
Wild eyes and nostrils rearing high
But hindlegs sunk deep in black rock

The toad that lunges from the far
Horizon, jaws apart as though to croak
Is swallowing the sky—

It almost fits into his gullet

The raging horse is nearly free.

Inviolable

Horse, huge
On the hilltop
Leaning

Massy chest
To the open sky,
Unhaltered sun,

Meadows and
The hankering sea
Embracing —

O great
Creatures I would clasp
And nuzzle

Over the barbed
Wire fence
Though I trespass

My boundaries,
Breaking
Your laws.

First Flight

I watches me climb
in the cockpit, him fixing
the belt and waving
my hand I see

the prop rev and the plane
cough forward
both wings biting
sudden wind

I on ground invisible
sees me taxi obvious
behind him Wild Pilot
what I doing there & here

particularly when
up high he says
Dan,
he says, Dan boy,

take over I don't feel
too good after all
that Scotch-type rot
last night I'm flying

me at the joystick o
boy how come
those chickens getting bigger chasing
their shadows under stoops

I see it clearly
clearly
STICK BACK!
and we climb

higher than the sun
sinking in a stew of clouds
Well Major anything
for a laugh me say

I say let's bring her down

A Solitary

Oblique essence of the personal,
Your individuality's a hanged man on the neck
Of an albatross. O let the bird fly free,

That wide-winged soul has never
Shot a quill at you,
Murderer of your double!

Lacking companion, now
Exulting that you are unique,
You stake your camp on spiritual territory,

Not the human. Self-contemplation
Must be the range of your philosophy,
O bleak essence of the personal.

The Companion

Whether we come, in last imaginings,
To our earliest unremembered dream,
Or at the end it's still discovery,
Always the conquest of a final shore,

He will be waiting for me there,
As ever second-sighted and first there:
I groping my way in radiant day,
He cleaving midnight quick as flame;

He owns my features, favored gaunt as I,
Good luck's all his, yet he takes mine with me.
My tedious failures he disowns,
No place I triumph but it is his home.

'He was the first who had returned'

He was the first who had returned
From that country
Of another tongue.

Speech, there,
Used purer forms of ecstasy than love
Here. Our actions fumble
With a gross vocabulary.

He makes the world
Around him glow
In simplicity of light.
His nouns are proverbs but their wisdom lies

Useless
In our boroughs of necessity,
Pure homage
Only known
When blood has crumpled, all its glories gone.

The Last Arrival

The last arrival in the furthest country,
All he saw he saw as mystery.
He to doorknob, counterpane and incised stone
That chanced to notice him appeared
Too familiar for comment.

And so they got used to one another,
The mysteries and the familiar.
In time all mysteries became familiars.
He in long familiarity
Disowned their secrets of their mystery.

Ceasing to notice him, they left as though
By prearrangement for the nearest country.
Someone will be the first to find that country,
In reciprocity for its reality
Will learn new names of all the mysteries

And write such full particulars in letters home
Unlike all correspondence known,
Since he with counterpane, doorknob and cut stone
Will parse that language of their own
To blurt out mysteries in ours, where all's familiar.

'When my wiser brother'

When my wiser brother
Who speaks so rarely
And only in my voice

(He is too busy matching souls
To the trees they will resemble, lovers
With one another,
The seahorse and the sun,
Sweet labor,
There's little time for speech)—when he

Finds words
Acceptable I will declare him,
For I am ready:
My phonemes, signs, parentheses
Await his spell.

All will be well
Disposed to consecrate the map
Of new peninsulas he will bequeath me.
But just when I've stepped out to choose the wine
For the banquet of our fond reunion
He will be gone,
Off to that republic
Of pure possibility
Where he plots a *coup d'état* against my exile.
Sometime, he may reveal it,

Though I am left meanwhile
Unbrothered,
My words all fled from split cicada skins
Into a busy fraction of the day.

The Way He Went

He didn't go away
To the roll of drums
Or to annuciatory thunder
Of mantic voices,

He didn't leave by the long light
Of line-storms slashing doomed horizons
Or the guiding blink and dousing
Of little harbor lights,

He went by darkness and by daylight going
A silent way
Vacating endless
Acreages of parking-lots and marshes

Still
Then evening all atwitch with raucous birds
Ignorant of the emptiness that fell
Lighter than dew.

He went
And the stars shone hard and rocks
Arose in their accustomed risings
From the sea while broken clouds

Scudded around and closed against
Ragged towers of a city
Gathering tumults of electric signboards
Glowing in the sky where many colors

Made one color
As before.

The Victor

When the fight was over
And the enemy lay dead
The victor shuddered in a daze,
Holding the butchered head

Of one whose strength had all but matched his strength,
Whose wile he undid by his guile.
Proven, his own superiority.
Still he quakes, tasting in victory

Blood hated, yet prized.
He had put on
That murderous character, in foe despised,
And how suck air in innocence again?

Lines for Jack Clemo

                    author of *The Map of Clay*,
                    now blind and deaf,
                    a 'Prisoner of God'

I stand on gritty Goonamarris,
The four elements assail me.
How can my senses hold all Nature's
Clarity and the soil of man?

He, leonine before the firescreen, paces
The kingdom of deprivation's borders
Striking the stones to make them sing.
No land's so bleak he cannot find those stones:

His Adversary guards the glazed ground.
They wrestle head to head and wound to wound,
Then inward darkness burns away,
Shards of silence frame the essential psalm.

The Wastrel

This blear-eyed sun
Lurches down the horizon's
Street, deserted, cold.
He is himself the dull

Penny he beseeches.
Will no one help to fill
His empty cup?
Who'd think his gaze was golden

When he mounted up
The morning's tower of glass—
Then poised at the very top,
Profligate in air,

It was himself that made
What's paltry or despised
Resemble him. Each blade
Of grass he swathed in grace,

Dust blessed him to his face.
Dung shone in benison.
Who could forget that noon!
Yet who brings him its light

Now that his battered head
Totters down the road,
Or will repay the debt
Owed to spent delight?

Keys

As the days grow shorter many keys
Hang from our chains—
Keys to boxes, drawers, trunks, and rooms
Filled with trunks and drawers
And boxes, keys to vaults and keys to houses,
Heavy keys of wrought-iron, filed
To fit the doors we can't remember closing.
Keys that seem unlike our own
Keys that we would open gates with.
Walking through the aery corridors and gates
Ever ajar,
The road ahead unbarred and open
—See, if we turn
Around, the way lies
Behind us. We could go
Back down the very lanes we've been
Where nothing's changed,
Had we the one
Key that doesn't
Hang from these heavy chains.

The Summerhouse

Climbed uphill to the seashore summerhouse,
Domed and shingled cottage occupied
By certain predecessors in whose pots
Our porridge bubbles merrily. The waves
Crash beyond the windows. Without ceremony
They pack their things and are about to go.
Well, we will soon forget them walking
Dourly without shadows two by two.
It's our vacation, sheets dried in the sun—
Out from the floorboard, underneath the bed
With slightest scrape of scale on wooden grain
The flattened head of a silent copperhead
—A kitchen cleaver leaps into my hand,
Shining through the high song of your fear
The whacking silver arc of light descends
And head rolls, chomping, and the lithe
And lovely diamonds down the back writhe.
He, he, tall, returns, removes
A curved and grooved tooth and squeezes it
Into my palm.—'Here, it's yours now.'—'Thanks,
But might I not, as a memento, keep
The head?'—'Oh, no, there's poison in the fangs.'
And now he's dropped the snake into his thermos
Of iced tea ('The place is yours') and driven
Down the sinuous twisting distant road.
And we've the sunny, salty, freshened air
And wind-dried linen sheets to spread.

The Tale-Teller

Imagining a Father
Telescoped by time and distance nearer,
Larger, sitting at the bed's edge
—Beyond the sill the humpbacked branches
Conspire in cloaks; the gasping moon
Mints shadows on a desert floor—
But then the third wish of the seventh son,
A spindly cowherd with a knee of kibes
Who wears his good luck like a warm great-coat,
Flings open all the dormers and the night breathes
Companionable fragrance of new bread.
Branches flutter bannerets of birdsong.
The raggedy goosegirl claims her minion now
In golden gown and crown and silver shawl,
In all that empire theirs the one true fiefdom. All
That glowed between the grassblades and the moon
Grew luminous with love that spilled from them.
That's how the story ends. They loved each other
And their love like dew rejoiced the kingdom
And the teller of their tale
Was larger, nearer,
And his word was real.

Another Country

Coming to a cavern in a valley,
Who would not explore?
His pineknot lit, he thrust a way
Past droppings on the mossy floor,
Past walls that gleamed and streamed with waters
Into a chamber none had known before
Save who drew in colors deep as blood
The great creatures on that sacred dome
—Horned Huntsman, and the Woman, Moon—
It was then he found the doorway
To another country. Darkness
There is brighter than familiar noon.
The light that lights that land's like lightning.
Its sudden crackle rends the skies.
                                        He tries
To tell a prospect of that country,
His words as much like lightning as the mutter
Of seared cloud
When the bolt's dazzle has come, and gone.

'It cannot come because desired'

It cannot come because desired,
It makes
Its own weather, its own time
Glowing
Like the phosphorescent wake
Of ships,
Mysterious tumult
Slitting the sensuous sea.

Love does not know
How we retrace
Together our most desperate seeking
Our most sacred place;

It's with these
Banal bodies
That we must
Make do,
Their strangely bulged and cherished
Curvatures, their folds, their flanks,
Their impermanent
Ageing surfaces
Concealing

Messages that we
Discover, each
The other's own
Rosetta Stone—

Love, I never hear
The brusque unpurposed clamor of the street
Or breathe the damp
Dolor that floods our city from the vast
Cool vats of space
But hold, an amulet against mischance,
Remembrance of your touch,
Your hands, your urgent hips,
The imperishable light, your sleeping face.

A Marriage

'Remember that farmer down in Maine
Who said to us, "I've been
An abandoned island
Since she's gone"?

—That's the hurt of proud flesh
We've known,
The heart's self-borne contagion
When you or I have parted us

With those rending, furious
Irretrievable accusations.
Each gulp of air keeps the wound fresh.
Left to the individual freedom

Of broken ends
We can't make meet, I roar
Off, a space-bound satellite
With no earth to encircle, adrift

In that unfinished void
Where nothing numbs the red scar
Of a burnt-out asteroid.
And yet I turn, seeking some tremor

Of your light,
Your heat,
Wherever in that emptiness
You are.'

'Who was it came'

Who was it came
Over the mountains bearing
Gifts we did not ask?

—Not the sapience of the thrush
Or the ant's perdurance,
Something a body might use—

Who was it brought
Cerements and a wrinkled skin,
A sour digestion

Over the mountains, offering
Crotchets and a rheumy gaze
And wits gone wandering?

Just when we thought to repossess
The taut frenzies of Chicago jazz
And bridal ardor

Here he comes,
Inexorable gaffer in an old hat
Croaking our names.

Another Border

Was it we who stumbled
Unawares across a border
Into a bleaker diocese,

Or did October's camouflage
Of crisp and primal colors
Infiltrate the parish of our pleasures?

No matter now
Who crossed whom, these colder
Wizened days that crowd us

And you and I
Thrusting impatient through their shorter
Gaps of lessened light

Move forward
Toward another border
—It must be there

Awaiting us,
That apostolic territory
To which we go.

From
Broken Laws (1970)

Aphrodite

How could she come to us inviolate
From that uncomplicated country
Of pure feeling? History

Alters all it touches,
And if her image now is such
That we cannot know

Which sacred objects her slim hands
Held, still, her glance,
Resting a moment on our eyes,

Stays, then quickens with clamorous beat
The bursting heart abandoned to desire . . .
If some goatherd with his rude

Mattock, or pillager's keen sword
Gash the cover of her mound
To seize her, as though mortal,

From memory's chamber underground,
The imperfections of her image
Are not her imperfections, the scarred

Seam, the limb sheared
By avid diggers or the gnaw
Of vandal centuries. Her face

Requites the tribute of our awe,
Her body's lithe, incomparable grace
Drives imagination wild

Should it please her to appear
As the one in whose embrace
The love that is engendered is beguiled.

A Fortune

'All that I see is framed
On this one card. A reaper,
Bent, his gleaming blade unswung
And the grain like hair in the wind
Rippling, bent
Motionless, for the wind that moves it
Does not move. The sun,
Yes, the sun burns
An eyehole in metallic blue,
Pours a tunnel of shade
Beneath a foreground tree. There
The thighs, breasts,
Shoulders, face of a girl gleam
As though by moonlight
And the tree bursts
Into flower, the pattern
Of the petals intricate
As birdsong and her white
Arms reaching, reaching out . . . The slant
Horizon hangs
Above you curtaining a throne-room
Where the Queen of Hearts
Holds in her fierce grip
A sceptre like a sword.
On this bloodblack card
The silence
Swells with her exultance,
Her exactions.'

Over the rim

Of this day hovers
The just design
This day tried
But failed to find,
All its busy creatures

Spurting with desires,
Spieling the recipes
Of their self-justifications
By which the mind
Of the entire world

This day betrayed
The perfection of our common
Lot, our clearest thought
Into these fragments, these
Wounds, self-serving anthems

And ridiculous longings—among them
You and I were for a moment
Together welded in a semblance
Of what this broken
Day left unattained.

In the Graeco-Roman Room

I have seen 21 beautiful and naked
Aphrodites, each one arching
her small right foot, her slender
arms clasping the shift of wind
against her breasts. One can desire
what may scarcely be believed in,

one can admire the dozen Hercules
and Herakleses, archaic heroes
of the unprotected private parts,
so strong the skins of their
flayed lions seem
to grow from their own shoulders

—these, the idols of an Age of Error.
Not to be said, though, of the bronze
mouse 1¼
inches high blowing
a trumpet, one small paw and elbow
stopping his own ears.

A Trip

Our tickets
won't be honored
on this line?

But we've paid
full fares—
Look, we've brought

our lunches, packed
in paper bags
—And who are these

who take our places
singing, in the long
steel cone?

At the countdown
we stand
numbed

as castaways
On Turtle
Rock who watch

their frigate's sails
shrink to specks,
then nothing

where the sea
becomes the infinite
unfeatured blue.

A Special Train

Banners! Bunting! The engine throbs
In waves of heat, a stifling glare
Tinges the observation-car

And there, leaning over the railing,
What am I
Doing in the Orient?

Blackflies, shrapnel-thick, make bullocks
Twitch. The peasants stand
Still as shrines,

And look, in this paddy
A little boy is putting in the shoots.
He's naked in the sunlight. It's my son!

There he is again, in that
Field where the earth-walls meet.
It's his play-time. See, his hands are smeared

With mud, and now his white
Back is flecked with ash, is seared
By embers dropping from the sky—

The train chuffs past. I cry
Stop! Stop! We cross another paddy,
He's there, he's fallen in the mud, he moans my name.

A Natural Philosopher

This was a grand passion with him—
Knowing. He took all the things he knew
And wrote down all the things
He knew about those things
He gave them numbers for each property
With decimals to the seventh place and names

When everything he knew was named and numbered
The whole collection
Of the images of things in ranks of file drawers
Went dead
Dead as a xerox machine with the cord pulled

He couldn't even get
Copies of the copies
His mind had made
And as for feelings well the fire
Of curiosity that set him
Alight to begin with

Soaring toward the Empyrean gagged
On the emptiness of æther
As the hot rain of his abashed
Desire—it was after all expressing
This in the only language known
To a sensibility flawed by the pulling-
Out of the magnetic
Cord and still he tried he made the whole contraption
Of the universe the object
Of his intellectual love—

Fell upon him
From a sky of ashes

A Historian

The dead again
Burst from their levelled graves
They reassemble on the hill
Ready for disastrous victory
Where a great empire fell
On its foe and fell

Again in the hot wide
Landscape of his mind
The captains sit astride
Their festooned chomping horses send
Batallions into certain
Enfilade

O they can never
Change the outcome they have fought
This battle over
Never knowing
Why they are there
Still following

Tattered pennants ignorant
Of trade routes or the pride
Of prince or diplomat whose ruse
Charges them to ride
The bloodspecked foaming crest
Of this riptide

No more than he can know
The soldier's brute obedience to orders
The captain's fealty to the general's plan
The comanders wrapped in webbed illusion
That their strategy will follow
Their will

Nor know the iron taste of fear
In throats that do not seem a part
Of the same contraption as the legs
Wildly going their own way
Or the gut that retches at the smell of blood
Or the heart

Booming its dark cannonade
Until the heartbeat or the battle ends.
The tallying of losses starts again.
The sky thickens with buzzards' wings.
They settle, gorge, and circle, waiting for
The future

A Dreamer

Awakened by the clarity of dream
As the train pitched forward in a rush careening
Down the mountain—Who wouldn't scream
When brakes fail and the conductor
Leaps from hurtling car? It was good,
Good to clutch the reasonableness of terror,
There was reassurance in that real
Fall, real crags, a landscape of sensible
Disaster, not this nameless, numb
Dread, the humming sun a poisoned stinger.

A Marked Man

He has this wound
Like an open mouth
He keeps it hidden
A hand cupped on a scream

But it's there just the same
When he's in the bleachers
Or sits at the bar
Like a lipless mouth it's

Moaning his name

A distinguishing mark
For each gaze in the ballroom
All eyes in the ballpark
Why would they look somewhere else?

It doesn't seem likely
To close up in a pale stitch
And knit itself cured
Without a word

For whenever it's almost
About to grow sound
He's liable to poke a finger
Back in the wound

Which moans thereupon
An open mouth
He has this mark
I could tell you about

A Casualty

Ever since he arrived in this country
From a warmer climate
A more constant light

Had difficulty breathing.
After all the years
Not even this clemency of the weather

Makes it better.
Certain cells
Are dying, and the body's

Tolerance for liquids, foods
Declines, for medicaments, for air.
No tolerance for pleasure

As the exfoliations of the nerve-ends
By a lifetime's effort disciplined
To fine discriminations of desire

Twitch—now their ghosts
Throb in fire
Beyond the charred stumps of feelings.

Nobody's love can reach
Into the purity
Of such isolation.

In the instant of his pain's surcease
He recalls as in a rearview mirror
A pheasant glimpsed beside the road

His fender struck last summer
Half its feathers
Scattered like a fallen cloud

In convulsive trials to rise
Wildly unable just to acquiesce to
What glazed the golden pupils of its eyes.

A Waking

The fact that the sun has once again with sharp claws
Pried
Open the eye of the day
Does not establish
The necessity
Or recurrence
Of any of the terms

Like light or day and
Night we awaken
Knowing
That where we've been has led us only
To the edge
Of this field

And at our backs
Memories
Stolid as boulders cracked
By long-forgotten frozen rains
Do not advance
Toward the grackles
Whose strident plaint proclaims
Dominion
Of the dew

Resolution

A single egg hatched every shape that swarms.
The hand that ordained Chaos made the Forms.

Northern Lights

        Projected X-rays
         Of the frac
                tured
           Skull
         His perfect
     Sphere's flaw
           Schismatic
                    Ghostly
         Beautiful

Snow

It is as though the thought of angels fell
Ejaculating from a cloud
The syllables congeal in near
Aluminum skies
To this spindrift our footsteps bruise

February

The ignorant sun
Shone, shone in winter
Despite the winter
And the starved wind,

The sun burnishing
The wind, the wind
Clenching the sun—
Such the contention

Between these two.
We who walk here
Numbed in the bright blast
Crunch toward summer's blue.

Thaw

What tracks the night made
Wane upon the morning's melting
Brighter as they go

An April

An April we could hardly tell from May
Even the condensations trailing Superconstellations
In exigent monoxide overhead
Seem festive
Pennants waving ever
So slightly from the one horizon
3600 lbs per hour of waste
Slick wafting in irreversible
Smear
Across the day's unwitting smile

Summer Solstice

Who's to tell the night heron
This night merits his observation
Or inform the carpenter bee
Of the day's singularity?

Only the membrane in the tissue
Of the algae or the eye
Steeped in ancestral memory
Retentive of stimuli

Has that calendrical
Instinct by which in France
On this day children strew the road with petals
Men burn a paper goat the women dance

Singing

This season
Belongs to the creatures
Peepers claim the nights

Sparrow thrush and skreaking waxwing
Extrapolate toward morning
Their cadenzas of a gilded day

Instinctual calls whose importunity
Pleases, as though the webbed
Desirous song and aubade of the swamp sparrow

Were notes that we remembered singing
Once, and yearn after
Recollecting how to sing

The Sounds

No use to make a tape
Recording of the liftoff
Or incorporate the sounds

The oil rig emits
In our suite—not
These the true ground

The ordained cadences
For rendering the thought
Which music is

Suggested by vestigial
Bird's whistle now or wailed
Snatch on boy's harmonica

This Silence

In this silence
Hear the breathing
Mouths that suckle

At the breast
Of night—
Is it the wind now

Or the glint of their
Exhalations tousling
Trees across

Whose faces brim
The milky
Rivulets

I am the Sun

I am the sun the sun says
All that's scorched beneath my eye
Is mine   We were just going the winds sigh
What will become of us the leaves cry

Nowhere to go mutters the maple
Grizzled in its skin of wrinkles
What will become of us the lovers
Do not think to wonder in the dappled

Sun thrust through the wind-tossed leaves
Where head on breast and thigh at rest on thigh
Find such delight they'd take the world for love's
Body that cannot change or die

Aubade

Weaned from moon
By whitening sky

The still cove
Swells as the tide fills

There is no quenching water's
Thirst for light

Snatches for Charles Ives

All those long dead New England farm boys
Sprang unarmed from R. W. Emerson's brain.
Where they fell they since have lain,
We forgot them like an old song out of mind,

Forgot their succor by the roadside spring,
Their probities before an angry God.
That upright Judge they judged them by is gone.
And who recalls the beehive hymnal drone

Uplifted souls made as they made concord?
What joy they found who found joy in the Word!
What martial airs were theirs, the fifetune boy's
Calliope that piped them, gay in blue

Files toward those backgrounds of ripped trees
And shattered waggons we've seen in Brady's
Photographs . . . They lie there where they've fallen,
All tent fires out, all camaraderies forgotten.

Torchlight parades! Magnetic energy of crowds!
Temperance and Tippecanoe! All those causes
Lost for long, dwindling with memory's losses,
Restored by these wild chords and sweet discords.

From
The Center of Attention (1974)

After God

> 'The Jews have a Fancy, that when our Almighty Creator befpangled the Heavens with the *Stars of Night*, He left a Space near the Northern Pole, unfinifhed and unfurnifhed, that if any *After-God* fhould lay claim to Deity, a challenge to fill up that fpace might Eternally confute it.'
> —Cotton Mather

Who keeps his ceaselessly attentive eye
Upon the flight and fall
Of each Polaris through the wide feast-hall
Of the sky,
So like the life of man from dark
To dark in a little space,

Who in this bowling alley spins
Balls of light
At the back of the North Wind
Careening as their plastic skins
Mirror widdershins
Our sponsored images,

Who flings bright strands of platinum hair
And unpointed needles wandering
Through the frozen stratosphere
In a confusion
Of jagged rays
Until True North is lost,

Who deafens Aurora Borealis
With climbing fire,
Who spurts with the desire
That blazes and subsides in ashen
Droppings of contagion
After the whirlwind,

Him we beseech
As adepts who would scan and preach
The Providences of His will.
Be done, send us a sign
That we may read
By the shrivelled light of our gelded sun

The sentence of our sufferings.
His blood flames now
Against the Northern sky.
He walks among us, visible.
The next dawn brings
A vacant hour that sacrifice can fill.

The Twentieth Century

A squad of soldiers lies beside a river.
They're in China—see the brimmed gables piled
On the pagoda. The rows of trees are lopped
And the Chinese soldiers have been stopped
In their tracks. Their bodies lie
In bodily postures of the dead.

Arms bound, legs akimbo and askew,
But look how independently their heads
Lie thereabouts, some upright, some of the heads
Tipped on their sides, or standing on their heads.
Mostly, the eyes are open
And their mouths twisted in a sort of smile.

Some seem to be saying or just to have said
Some message in Chinese just as the blade
Nicked the sunlight and the head dropped
Like a sliced cantaloupe to the ground, the cropped
Body twisting from the execution block.
And see, there kneels the executioner

Wiping his scimitar upon a torso's ripped
Sash. At ease, the victors smoke. A gash
Of throats darkens the riverbed. 1900. The Boxer
Rebellion. Everyone there is dead now.
What was it those unbodied mouths were saying?
A million arteries stain the Yellow River.

Dark of the Moon

Squinting through smoked glass, the moon
Ate up her father and the boy
Shuddered as the glowering sky became
All smoke, no flame.
He heard no more the heartsick folks' sedition
Against something—the Market, the gov'ment—
No cadenzas on the shrunken dollar's dispossessions
That day, only, on that foreshortened day,
The startled clamor of unready birds.

After four decades the affluent sun
Again takes momentary shelter.
Now its full face is covered
In living color. The satellite, all systems
GO on schedule, moves, giving
A rare view of the corona as the camera
Swings to shoot the crowd in Mexico
—Indians, bare-eyed, gaping—then invisible
Enzymes power an automated wash.

The Center of Attention

As grit swirls in the wind the word spreads.
On pavements approaching the bridge a crowd
Springs up like mushrooms.
They are hushed at first, intently

Looking. At the top of the pylon
The target of their gaze leans toward them.
The sky sobs
With the sirens of disaster crews

Careening toward the crowd with nets,
Ladders, resuscitation gear, their First
Aid attendants antiseptic in white duck.
The police, strapped into their holsters,

Exert themselves in crowd-control. They can't
Control the situation.
Atop the pylon there's a man who threatens
Violence. He shouts, *I'm gonna jump*—

And from the river of upturned faces
—Construction workers pausing in their construction work,
Shoppers diverted from their shopping,
The idlers relishing this diversion

In the vacuity of their day—arises
A chorus of cries—*Jump!*
Jump! and *No*—
Come down! Come down! Maybe, if he can hear them,

They seem to be saying *Jump down!* The truth is,
The crowd cannot make up its mind.
This is a tough decision. The man beside me
Reaches into his lunchbox and lets him have it.

Jump! before he bites his sandwich,
While next to him a young blonde clutches
Her handbag to her breasts and moans
Don't   Don't   Don't   so very softly

You'd think she was afraid of being heard.
The will of the people is divided.
Up there he hasn't made his mind up either.
He has climbed and climbed on spikes imbedded in the pylon

To get where he has arrived at.
Is he sure now that this is where he was going?
He looks down one way into the river.
He looks down the other way into the people.

He seems to be looking for something
Or for somebody in particular.
Is there anyone here who is that person
Or can give him what it is that he needs?

From the back of a firetruck a ladder teeters.
Inching along, up up up up up, a policeman
Holds on with one hand, sliding it on ahead of him.
In the other, outstretched, a pack of cigarettes.

Soon the man will decide between
The creature comfort of one more smoke
And surcease from being a creature.
Meanwhile the crowd calls *Jump!* and calls *Come down!*

Now, his cassock billowing in the bulges of Death's black flag,
A priest creeps up the ladder too
What will the priest and the policeman together
Persuade the man to do?

He has turned his back to them.
He has turned away from everyone.
His solitariness is nearly complete.
He is alone with his decision.

No one on the ground or halfway into the sky can know
The hugeness of the emptiness that surrounds him.
All of his senses are orphans.
His ribs are cold andirons.

Does he regret his rejection of furtive pills,
Of closet noose or engine idling in closed garage?
A body will plummet through shrieking air,
The audience dumb with horror, the spattered street . . .

The world he has left is as small as toys at his feet.
Where he stands, though nearer the sun, the wind is chill.
He clutches his arms—a caress, or is he trying
Merely to warm himself with his arms?

The people below, their necks are beginning to ache.
They are getting impatient for this diversion
To come to some conclusion. The priest
Inches further narrowly up the ladder.

The center of everybody's attention
For some reason has lit up a butt. He sits down.
He looks down on the people gathered, and sprinkles
Some of his ashes upon them.

Before he is halfway down
The crowd is half-dispersed.
It was his aloneness that clutched them together.
They were spellbound by his despair

And now each rung brings him nearer,
Nearer to their condition
Which is not sufficiently interesting
To detain them from business or idleness either,

Or is too close to a despair
They do not dare
Exhibit before a crowd
Or admit to themselves they share.

Now the police are taking notes
On clipboards, filling the forms.
He looks round as though searching for what he came down for.
Traffic flows over the bridge.

The Translators' Party

The great Polish
Emigré towered
Over the American
Poets at the party
For the contributors
Who'd wrested and wrought
The intractable consonants
Of Mickiewicz
Into a sort
Of approximate English,

Tilll Auden went over
To Jan Lechon,
Half a foot taller
Than the rest of us scribblers
And would-be reviewers,
Those venerables
For an hour reliving
A continent's culture,
Aperçus in the lilting
Accents heard

In cafés in Warsaw,
Vienna, Kracow . . .
One with the fiction
Of civilized discourse
In his native diction
Still entertainable
In imagination,
The other among
Aliens, aliens
In an alien tongue

For whom the greatness
Of the poet Adam
Mickiewicz can only
Be indirectly
Expounded, like Chopin's
Shown in slide-lectures
To a hall of wearers

Of battery-powered
Audiophones,
For whom his own poems

Cannot be known but
In deaf-and-dumb hand-signs,
No shades of his sounds, his passionate
Rhythms twisted.
His poems are stateless.
Yet it's Lechon's laughter
That I remember,
With one who could summon
A world lost in common
For an hour's reversal

Of an age's disaster
—Never known
To us in our *Times*
A fortnight after
Who read he was found
'Apparently fallen'
From his high window,
That voice
Stilled now
On New York's alien ground.

The Princess Casamassima

After digging in the rubble of the ruined house
For nine days
They've found a *third* corpse —
No fingerprints; no hands.
One leg and the head blown off.
The story in the *Times*
Didn't even tell
The sex of the torso . . .

These were some of the people
Who'd take power to the people
In their own hands.
All their questions have one answer.
Dynamite
Makes non-negotiable demands
For an apocalypse,
In case of survivors.

Once, another world ago,
There was a girl I never dreamed
Would be like them:
She seemed to lack nothing
— Looks, friends, certainly a silver
Spoon had stirred her porringer —
She'd sit scribbling
Notes in the next to the back row,

But I can't remember now
One word she wrote for me.
— Good God,
Was it something *I* said
About Thoreau
Shorted her fuse? Oh,
Such unbalanced, mad
Action is surely extra-curricular —

If the discourse of our liberal arts
Which entertains all rival truths as friends
And rival visions reconciles
Could but bring the pleasures of its wholeness
To a mind

Rent by frenzy—
But how conceive what hatred
Of the self, turned inside-out, reviles

The whole great beckoning world, or what desire
Sentenced the soul
To that dark cellar where all life became
So foul
With the pitch of rage,
Rage, rage, rage to set aflame
Father's house—what can assuage
That fire or that misfire?

Power

'My life is a one-billionth part
Of history. I wish I was dead.'

He rips the page from his notebook.
Litter in a rented room.

The neighbors will barely remember
His silence when they said Hello.

They'll not forget his odd smile.
Nobody comes to see him.

When he thinks of his folks he smiles oddly.
'It was broken but was it a home?'

At night, the wet dream. Arising,
He is afraid of women.

In his notebook, 'Power over people!'
His job, scouring pots in a hash-house.

At last he will pick up a girl.
She'll think, Does he ever need love—

But I don't like him at all.
Her Mom will hang up on his phone call.

One day he will fondle a snub-nosed
Pistol deep in his pants.

What is his aim? The TV,
Even bumper stickers remind him

Who has the face and the name
His name and smile will replace.

His trigger will make him bigger.
He will become his victim.

When he steps from his rented room
History is in his hands.

The Sonnet

(Remembering Louise Bogan)

The Sonnet, she told the crowd of bearded
    youths, their hands exploring
        rumpled girls,
        is a sacred

vessel: it take a civilization
    to conceive its shape or know
        its uses. The kids
        stared as though

a Sphinx now spake the riddle of
    a blasted day. And few,
        she said, who would
        be *avant-garde*

consider that the term is drawn
    from tactics in the Prussian
        war, nor think
        when once they've breached

the fortress of a form, then send
    their shock troops yet again
        to breach the form,
        there's no form—

. . . they asked for her opinion of
    'the poetry of Rock.'
        After a drink
        with the professors

she said, This is a bad time,
    bad, for poetry.
        Then with maenad
        gaze upon

the imaged ghost of a comelier day:
    I've enjoyed this visit,
        your wife's sheets
        are Irish linen.

Print-Out Song

AND his dark secret love
O rose, thou ART sick!
Has found out thy BED

Of CRIMSON joy.
And his DARK secret love
Does thy life DESTROY.

DOES thy life destroy.
That FLIES in the night
Has FOUND out thy bed

HAS found out thy bed
And HIS dark secret love
In the HOWLING storm

That flies IN the night
IN the howling storm
The INVISIBLE worm

Of crimson JOY.
Does thy LIFE destroy.
And his dark secret LOVE

That flies in the NIGHT
O rose, thou art sick!
OF crimson joy

Has found OUT thy bed
O ROSE, thou art sick!
And his dark SECRET love

O rose, thou art SICK!
In the howling STORM
THAT flies in the night

THE invisible worm
That flies in THE night
In THE howling storm

O rose, THOU art sick!
Has found out THY bed
Does THY life destroy.

The invisible WORM

132

O Personages

O Personages who move
Among me, why don't you
Guys come on call?
How can I serve the lost
King who, when the Secret
Service infiltrate the Ball Park
And the would-be assassin
Is paralyzed by the beams
Of their binoculars,
Paddles his paper-birch canoe
Where the sun's blood drowns the sea?

Musebaby, what good are you to me
In the dark spirit of the night?
Who needs you more than when the will,
Exhausted, finds dry clay
Where imagination's fountains were—dry clay;
O remorseless Goddess, you
Take your graces somewhere else.
Bleakness is bleak. And you,
Little Boy Blue in the velvet suit
My own Aunt Billie gave me when she came
Home from Vienna,

—You were fullsized, I was only three—
Where's that unquestioning insouciance
With which you bawled *Mine! Mine!*
Seizing all the candles on the birthday cake,
Eating them—Why do you fade
To brown, to tan, to nothing as
The rotogravure fades, leaving
Me alone with this bunch of motives
Scratching their armpits, gesticulating
From the crotches
Of leafless trees?

Comanches

Weak after long fasting, felt a slow
Trembling shake the earth—the buffalo!—
And raced their ponies barebacked toward the herd.
That morning not a brave in camp could gird
Himself with strength to bend the stout bowstem,
Yet with bursting arms he twangs his arrow
Deep in the bison's heart! Comanches know
The Great Spirit, when it possesses them.

And now the poet, half a savage bound
By the hungers of his tribe, paces his swift
Foray across a desolate hunting-ground
In hopes to run to earth a fleeting creature
And, with the unpremeditated gift
Of spirit, seize imagination's meat.

Brainwaves

When his head has been wired with a hundred electrodes
Pricked under the skin of his scalp and leading
Into the drum of intricate coils
Where brainwaves stimulate motion

In a finger so sensitive that it can trace
The patterns of idiosyncrasy
Which, without his knowing or willing,
Are the actions of his mind,

He is told to lie down on the cot and the current
Begins to flow from his brain through the hidden
Transistors. The needles on dials veer.
The finger makes a design.

The attendant is reading the dials: no more
Input than that from a distant star,
Its energy pulsing for millions of years
To reach the electroscope's cell.

He lies there thinking of nothing, his head
Hurting a little in so many places
He can't tell where. If the current reverses
Direction he'd be in shock,

But the pulsing of twitches and their subsidings
Flow toward squared paper. Is it good
For a man to be made aware that his soul
Is an electric contraption,

The source of his dreams a wavering voltage
From a battery cell—such a piece of work
That the stars in their circuits are driven through space
By an analogue of its plan?

Tree

This is a slice of the oldest
Tree the world has known.

When this outside ring grew in the forest
Chainsaws and a tractor brought it down.

When the tree's husk was this narrow ring,
Washington's troops were shivering;

In this ring's year the Tartar horde
Drenched earth with blood of the conquered;

In this year, a black ring—
As a cross was a tree hung;

Gilgamesh journeyed toward the dark
When this ring swelled beneath the bark;

When sap rose here the tree was great
With blossom, with unfallen fruit;

Here, fed by roots that reached far down
To suck milk out of the earth,

These heartwood rings grew firm. Their girth
Braced high boughs, and a spreading crown

Held unchanging stars as leaves;
The tree propped up the heavens

And gods drowsed in its shade
Then, before time was made.

These dates of interest are each marked now
On the cracked disc by a cardboard arrow.

Shrew

His heart has a quicker beat
Than the clitter of a frightened sandpiper's feet.

His life is a furious passage
Into the future which is today.

Relentless, he tracks his prey.
He would die in a night

Unless he eat
Twelve times his own weight.

His mouth of needles
Makes a cry

—If it could reach us his shrill
Shriek would terrify—

Kill! Kill! Kill!
He harrows the bug,

Grasshopper, grub,
Yet his belly's never full

Nor will he rest unless he hear
The noiseless prowl

And cocked ear
Of the circling owl.

Boar

In the mountains behind the chateau where no one could live
In the brambles and only brigands and Maquis would dare
To seek shelter, they are hunting the boar. They are blowing their horns
And beating their drums and making

A devilish din as the boarhounds run the scent deeper
Into the enemy forest. He's in a ravine now,
A steep defile, and the hounds are yelling and baying.
Blocking its mouth. The boar's

Hackles arise and a collar of nails bristles,
Protecting his jugular vein. His clumsy bulk
Dances on murderous hooves, in sudden lunges
And the scimitar tusks drip red

And a dog wails as its innards and voice fall
And the pack's baying is shredded by yelps of confusion
And fear. The savage will in this wild boar
With froth on his tushes was his

When a piglet, blind, he rooted for place at the teat.
It will be in the boar even after this hunt is over.
—He lunges again and another hound staggers and sobs
In its own blood. Their ardor

Is chilled by an ancient terror that stays the blood.
If the hunters with trumpets and guns dare step within range
Of those hooves and tusks they will know that single purpose
Of which this boar is steward.

Dogfish

He lurks and sidles away out of sight. But when you stand
At the rail of a cruiser twenty miles from land
Hauling the inert haddock and sluggish cod

Suddenly one, then two, three, four of the lines pull
Taut in a tangle, go slack and taut again with a caught
Life fighting in jerks and rushes deep under the keel,

Then in a battle of shouts, bent rods, and whirring reels
And curses and the pulling of lines in a net of knots
Tied together by a wild shuttle, alive and enraged,

He's gaffed and over the rail, slashing our boots with his tail,
A streak of muscle and will, writhing and gnashing until
The mate hands me the hatchet to hack his head off

—I see that struggle in the mind's slow motion still:
Dogfish, smallest of sharks, who just was the terror
That rocketed through the somnambulant schools

Of weakfish fated for his belly or our chowder,
His head atilt, the underslung jaw of sawblades ripping
White flesh in the deep green dimness.

A stinking gobbet of squid on my hook was
His undoing. Wedged in his ravenous throat
The barbed iron, the invisible cord, relentless.

My arm is unable to stop. I beat the blade
Where the gills writhe with a life of their own and the head
Flops free. His body as long as my arm jerks to a dead stop.

Blood

At a wolf's wild dugs
When the world was young
With eager tongue
Twin brothers tugged,

From foster mother
Drew their nurture.
Her harsh milk ran
Thence in the blood of man,

In the blood of kings
Who contrived the State.
What wolvish lust to lead the pack
The memory of that taste brings back.

Egg

Now that Robin Redbreast
Has dropped an egg into her nest,
Round as the horizon, blue
As Heaven is, O lucky Egg,
There's only four or five things that you
Need know how to do:

1. Learn to hack your way out
2. To grow up (and master flying)
3. Finding where the worms are
4. Copulation, etc., aerial
5. Nest-building skills

That's *it*. Everything else
Is optional, and who cares
For your opinions of your ancestors
Or views about the Great Redbreast
Who roosts at evening in the West?
The Future with its wrinkled brow
Will arrive regardless how
You try to flee, there is no place
But there it will reveal its face.
No more can you escape the dust
Than prove that Night, or Day, is just.
What's the use to weep or rage
Because all Heaven is a cage?
You have your how-to-do-it skills,
So don't peck at the world's ills.

Rats

To rid your barn of rats
You need a watertight
Hogshead two-thirds full
You scatter your cornmeal
On the water
Scattered as though all
The barrel held was meal
And lean a plank against the rim
And then lay down—

This is *important!*

—A wooden chip the size
To keep one rat afloat
He'll rid your barn of rats
He'll leap into your meal
He'll sink he'll swim and then he'll
See the chip
He'll slither aboard and squeal
And another rat beneath your eaves
Will stop
 and listen,

And climb down to that barrel
And walk that plank and smell
The meal and see meal
And one rat
He'll hear that rat squeal
I'll get mine he'll think and he'll
Leap in and sink and swim
He'll scramble on that chip

—Now watch him!—

He'll shove the first rat down
In the water till he'll drown
He'll rid your barn of rats
He'll shiver and he'll squeal
And a rat up on your rafter
Will hear,
 and stop,
 and start

Down the beam
Coming after
With one intent as in a dream—

He'll rid your barn of rats.

Eagles

When things are creatures and the creatures speak
We can lose, for a moment, the desolation
Of our being

Imperfect images of an indifferent god.
If we listen to our fellows then,
If we heed them,

The brotherhood that links the stars in one
Communion with the feathery dust of earth
And with the dead

Is ours. I have seen bald eagles flying,
Heard their cries. Defiant emblems of
An immature

Republic, when they spread their noble wings
They possess the earth that drifts beneath them.
I've learned how

Those savage hunters when they mate are wed
For life. In woods a barbarous man shot one
In the wing.

He fluttered to an island in the river.
After nearly half a year, someone,
Exploring, found

Him crippled in a circle of the bones
Of hen and hare his partner brought to him.
Close above,

She shrieked and plunged to defend her helpless mate.
Eagles, when they mate, mate in the air.
He'll never fly.

His festered wing's cut off, he's in the zoo.
They've set out meat to tranquillize his queen
And catch her too.

Who'll see them caged yet regal still, but thinks
Of eagles swooping, paired in the crystal air
On hurtling wings?

Burning Bush

If a bush were to speak with a tongue of fire
To me, it would be a briar;
The barberry, bearing unreachable droplets of blood,
Or, bristling in winter, rugosas with their red hoard

Of rosehips and a caucus of birds singing.
Come Spring, in a burst at the road's turn,
A snowblossom bank of the prickly hawthorn;
Or drooping in June on their spiny, forbidding stem

Blackberries ripe with the freight of dark juice in them.
If I should listen to a bush in flame
Announce the Unpronounceable Name
And demand requital by a doom

On my seed, compelling more
Than I'd answer for, what no one else would ask,
That voice of fire would blaze in a briar
I cannot grasp.

Shell

I would have left the me that was then
Clinging to a crack in the bark of the tree,

Stiffened in wind, the light translucent,
A brittle shell that had the shape of me;

And down the back a split through which had burst
A new creature, from mean appearance free,

Swaying now where the topmost boughs of the tree sway
At the center of the sound that's at the center of the day.

Wherever

North

For reasons of their own the red-winged blackbirds
Have gathered in a cloud. They fall like snow.

The skies, the trees, the fields are black with blackbirds,
Black with the pandemonium of their cries.

The only place more desolate than this one
Is this, when the last straggling birds have flown.

East

Always the mysterious
Promise of a new day.

This is the place
Of birth, the distant home

Of the future
God. Until he come

There is no entrance
There. What awaits us we

Can know only
By our deliverance.

South

Here you hoard the green
Hieroglyphs of morning
All the baffled afternoon.

West

You can journey toward it forever
Without arriving.
Each of your footsteps enlarges behind you
The lost land you seek.

The Wanderer

This body that has fastened
Itself to the wanderer

Who hastens with mysterious
Balked purposes,

These hands that answer,
This face that turns

At the calling
Of the name

That I am wearing
Like one shoe

—How did I come
In all this gear

Among so few
Clues to where I've come from

Or where
I am to go?

Runner

There's not enough air in the sky for his lungs to gulp
A full draught that would quench the heat in his blood.
His heart is about to pound apart and his legs
Are flogged slaves from a conquered country.
They've trodden the ground till they're numb.

He has run all morning and run while the sun in the heavens
Lurched to the top of its climb and hung, unmoving
All that long noon, spreading the drone of its heat
And all that while his dogged feet
Ran on in the dust, and ran

Past gates that opened and doors that tilted ajar
On quiet rooms and gardens where fountains sighed
And languorous women as the light streamed from their hair
Looked up with secretive smiles that said
'At last you've arrived here,'

Yet still he plods on though behind him his shadow grows
   longer
And the shadows of trees are meshed with their boughs and
   their trunks.
That unending road he treads in a narrow passage
—By night will he know that the path he follows
Is the earth's wheel, spinning and spinning?

Sickness

He becomes the terrain an enemy force
Advanced on, spread out and dug into,

Mounting artillery in his head.
Siege guns all night long.

Blinded by bloodshot, he can't get through
To his own HQ.

They've poisoned his well. His nerves
Have been sabotaged,

His body's a burned-out battlefield, burning.
There's little fight left in him.

He'd put out the white flag if he could
Discover to whom to surrender.

He'd clear out of here if he could
Only hold himself steady

—His back is shaking, his legs
Twitch like a stepped-on spider's.

He is drained, drained white,
White as a midnight frost

And then in a deep sleep it's all over.
Come morning, he's a new man.

Evening

As a corpse
Bleeds
In the presence of its murderers

The scars
Of this grey sky
Burst again,

The wounds
Gush. On our hands,
The stain.

A Dread

It can be practically nothing, the nearly invisible
Whisper of a thought unsaid.
Pulsing, pulsing

At the bland center of a blameless day
It spreads its filaments through the world's
Firm tissues,

Relentless as an infection in the blood
Of one's own child, or a guilt
Time won't assuage.

A Woe

Larger than the sky
That squats upon the vast horizon
There is a woe

Pressing down
On this house of stone.
It thickens in the air of this room.

It is as though
One loved as much—no, more—
Than oneself were trying

To thrust away
With small hands
Stifle of the heavy air

While in the dark
I lie
Pinioned, all my strength

Useless to prize
The weight of heaven
From her eyes.

Thought I Was Dying

Like a bucket
With a hole

I couldn't find
Just felt the seeping

Of my life
As it was leaving

My wife my children
Drifting away

My head empty
My hands my heart

Drained and void
The bed cold

I thought it's hard
To leave my life

With each breath
A little less

In the veins whistling
Till the sun shone black

As though I never
Could come back

Vows

I meet him in the spaces
Between the half-familiar places
Where I have been,
It's when I'm struggling toward the door
Of the flooded cellar
Up to my crotch in a cold soup
Of my father's ruined account books
There, like an oyster cracker
Floats my mother's Spode tureen
(The one they sold at auction
When the market was down)—

Then just outside
Before I'm in the trooptrain on the siding
Spending the vivid years
Of adolescence and the war
With dented messkit in hand
Always at the end
Of a frozen chowline
Of unappeased hungers,
He appears—

Listen, kid,
Why do you bug me with your reproachful
Silent gaze—
What have I ever
Done to you but betray you?
To which he says
Nothing.

Listen, I'd forget if I could
Those plans you made
For stanching the blood
Of the soul that spread
Its cry for peace across the unjust sky,
I wouldn't give it a thought if I

Could only not
Remember your vows
To plunge into the heat
Of the heart and fuse

With the passionate Word
All thought,
All art—

Come, let's go together
Into the burning
House with its gaping door.
The windows are all alight
With the color of my deeds,
My omissions.
It's our life that's burning.
Is it ever too late to thrust
Ourselves into the ruins,
Into the tempering flame?

Hang-Gliding from Helicon

I

Himself

The one most like himself is not this mirror's
Dishonest representation
Of a familiarly strange person

Growing more crinkled around the eyes,
But one on whom he has not set his eyes,
One he knows is in this house with him.

In this very room there is
A youth he has outgrown, whose ease
With the world is greater than his own,

Whose gifts are greater than his gifts,
Whose joys are deeper joys
Than any he has known.

By the time that he began
To grow apart from that potential grace
He had never worn its face,

His callow years were all a waste
Of foolish choices and false satisfactions.
The blessing given him at last

Across the alien years
Is that he now may judge his actions
By what that one most like himself would do

Whose ease with the world shames his unease,
Whose delights exceed the joys he's known,
Whose gifts are greater than his own.

His Steps

You can just about keep pace with his
Skulking steps or leaps that tread your steps,
His back a sliver or dark hump by your side.

No matter how quick, how long his gait is
How supple his torso or how far
He leans away from you at evening

He will come back like a wild brother,
Linked in the syncopations of the light
As stolid theme and impetuous cadenza

Dance to the measure of the one song,
Or as a dream of flight that dares
Not leave its dreamer for long.

A Stone

Plodding down the road, past
A standing stone, scored, not
With distance to a destination
But the number that proclaims
How far I've come. It's always
When the earth is springy after
First thaw and the golden
Trumpets of forsythia
Are about to blow, I pass it
Going where I have to go,
Toward a stone casting its shadow
Farther down the road, scored
With parentheses, cupped hands
Enclosing half an emptiness
That awaits its filling-in.

Folk Tale

It's enough to make one think they knew
Something, those old crones. At whose request
    Do they tweak baby's cheek with gnarled
Fingers? Who asked them, perched on every cradle,
To intone a blessing in their fireside cackle?
If we could only start out once without it—

Why is it that, when, as a new door opens
Toward an untried way stretching before us
    With limitless invitation, always
There's a staying hand weighs on the shoulder
The sharp restraint of that remembered blessing,
Their admonition, You'll be most nearly happy

With a box you never open. Who then
Can think of anything down the road, the windings
    Unexplored, the paths, the houses
Deep in the woods, the trees startled with birds
And all made radiant with expectancy
—Who then can think of anything save that box

Because forbidden? Now at such a time
The guests have all subsided, their bottles spent,
    The drowsy sun itself falls silent.
Then night concludes the gathering for all
Communicants save lover and beloved
Who depart for haven to fulfil

Those rites for which these steps and incantations
The others witnessed were preludial.
    At such a time a barred door
Tantalizingly can open—Now
May they recall the wisdom of the tribe
Before it is too late, before it is

Too late. Something it was about an open
Box. Or was it not to open? No matter,
    A meteor throbs, he thrusts its blaze
Into the darkness of the opening crack—
Her limbs melt, drops of tallow fall.
This is a tale that will be told again.

The Sacred Fount

Stubborn hidalgo, rusting in his mail,
Outliving enemies, his loves, his time.
What spell, what doom lures him to hope that Time,
Whose breath seres every limb, would leave him hale?

The stagnant swamps he's swigged! How many's the time
Since being gulled by a Medicine Man's tall tale
He's almost found that fount; but weary, frail,
An old dog can but piddle away his time.

Who hasn't hacked through mangroves, tried to suck
The juvenescent dew from the earth's breast,
Gulped potions, bottles, jugs, with just his luck

While Memory's daughter still holds out her Grail—
One taste, and a body is forever blessed,
She sings, from thickets serried as chain-mail.

Possession

You were sleeping? That's the time you're
Likeliest to hear my rat-tat-tat-tat-tat
Beat upon the pane between
Your self and your desire. The breeze

Baffling the leaves of your thought
Grows harsher, colder. This chill
Wind that clamps your veins
Is fanned from the black feathers

Of my outstretched wings. Of your wings.
Half-awake
You feel yourself reclaim the shape
You took before you took your shape.

Stop the Deathwish! Stop It! Stop!

—at least until the 21st century
because the present is too good to lose
a moment of—I would begrudge the time
for sleep, but dreams are better than they used
to be, since they enact the mystery
that action hides and history derides.
The past drains from the present like the juice
of succulent clams left in the noonday sun.
I spent the better part of my long youth
prenticed to arts for which there'll be small use
in whatever work the future needs have done:
I can file a needle to a point
so fine it plays three sides before it burrs,
or split a hundredweight of ice to fit
the cold chest with a week's worth in two blows;
is there many a man around who knows
by rote the dismantled stations of the El,
or that the Precinct House in Central Park
was once a cote from which the lambing ewes
and spindly lambs and crookhorned rams set out
to crop the green? In one-flag semaphore
I can transmit, or signal in Morse code
by heliograph such urgent messages
as scouts and sappers a boyhood ago
squinted through binoculars to read.
I still can cobble *rime royale* by hand
—and may, though now, about as few use rhyme
as wigwag or sun's mirrored beam to spell
their definitions of the ways that Time
endows the present it consumes, or tell
how only in this moment's flare we dwell
save when Memory, with her hands outspread,
brings back the past, like Lazarus, from the dead.

II

The Great American Novel

I have spent most of my life
Gathering material.

Autumn. I am learning to balance
My brand new bicycle. Under
The pin oak Father
At a collapsible table
Sits on a folding chair.

The tale is as long as the slow
Braiding of Mother's black hair.

No matter how often he harrows
His pencil down the columns
The total is always the same,
The same parentheses always
Signifying (Loss).

Asleep

Your Grammy's had pneumonia, a bad cold,
And now she's gone to sleep. We're going to town
To say good-bye to Grammy—we've a treat
For you, you'll spend the day
At Gussie's—? No, she won't wake up
For your birthday . . . We'll be late. They went
And left me with our courtesy maiden Aunt
In ground-gripper shoes and hat of suffragette
Who lived with sister Elsa—spinster, vague
Transcendentalist, her memory
A jumble-shop of buttons, lofty thoughts.
Tame at the feeders, birds on every sill
And great gold fish dreamed beneath the lilies
In the indoor and the outdoor pools. That day
Behind a laurel I found the polished stone
Lettered OUR LAD. Then, at the kitchen stoop
Aunt Elsa, head in duster, waved and called,
You've found our doggie sleeping? Come to the kitchen,
Dear, before it's time to go,
I'll give you what he likes—an old steak bone.
Heaving with sobs, head cradled on that stone,
The long day wracked with inexplicable loss,
I mourned a dog I'd never known.

A Barn Burnt in Ohio

The night whitened in the bubbling light that poured
Out of the Milky Way, and in the pines
The massed voices of a million peepers sang
Whatever it is the stars to each other are singing

And then the silken glowing air was jabbed and torn
By the hoarse bellow of klaxon, the howling
Of firetruck sirens. Doors slammed like shots
And the whole village rushed to follow

The high red pumper with wood-spoked wheels, the scream
Of that pitched horn stabbing the clapboard houses
And the La France ladder truck gleaming, swerving
Through turns in the road between the curving fences.

A mile in the woods we heard the astounded voices
Of old boards snapped and twisted by great heat,
Felt the gibbering shadows of frightened trees
Leap and duck and turn at the wind's least twist and turning,

Saw the barn aglow, the cracks between the sidings
Liquid with orange and molten light. Then roaring sawblades
Of fire ripped through the roof on a suck of wind
And a great bellows beat storms of flinders skyward

As helmeted brigades with squirting hoses shrank
Back, back from the heat that pulsed out from the barn,
The barn a black outline still rigid in the fluxion
Of uppouring firestorm, flecks of hot ash flung on

Flapping tents of fire beneath a whirlwind sky—
It's forty years now since the old barn burned
In Ohio, and there among the villagers, some long dead,
I still stand still, silhouetted by that pyre,

Stand as the barn stood once while snow, a century
Of snow swirled past its eaves, where snow, where ash,
Executors of time's changeless will,
Sift down, till memory lose that ruined doorsill.

High Society

'Toby's' in Cos Cob—faded mirrors, a smoked-wood bar
in an old roadhouse behind a row of trees,
still trading on the great ill fame
of those police raids years before.
Early, I sit at the table nearest the bandstand.
'Hey kid, better not let nobody
see ya drink that drink'—a great white
toothy smile, bulk of body heaving
in genial laughter, 'or you'll spend
the night in jail,' and the drummer tries
brushes on his snare. Cozy Cole
has talked to me! Now Art
Hodes puts his drink down carefully
in a coaster on the piano top and spreads
his left hand clear across a tenth, a twelfth,
riffles off some chords, as Max Kaminsky
—I'm a lot taller than he is—takes his seat,
warming the mouthpiece in one hand, the other
fingering the keys. Edmund Hall unpacks
his clarinet, fits the halves together, turns
the ridged nuts tightening his reed, then forms
his embouchure around the mouthpiece,
puts down the instrument and looks around,
sees me, transfixed to hear him play.
'Hiya kid, wasn't you at Nick's last Sat'day night?'
He remembers! Maybe he remembers
my telling him I'm trying to learn to play
like him . . . 'Listen, kid,
before we start' (the somber room is still,
nearly empty under glum electric gaslamps)
'Lemme show you what you gotta know
if you're gonna play like me. D'ja ever
hear the Picou Chorus?' And now my heart's
a leaden fishweight. All those hours
replaying stacks of records bought
from the jukebox depot for a quarter each
(school lunch skimped for weeks to save the quarters),
my hoard of Bluebirds, red Vocallions, scratched Okehs,
discards from ginmills up and down the Post Road,
and I never heard the Picou Chorus
so look a dummy, knowing nothing, to Ed Hall.

'Yeah, old Alphonse Picou's chorus
in "High Society" like I learned it
off Leon Rapallo who played it just
like old Alphonse Picou—He'd always play it,
even after he went off his nut
he'd play it all alone there in the bughouse
in N'Orleans. Somebody wants to play the clarinet
in N'Orleans, he's got to play that chorus. At your age
I could do it pretty good. It goes
like this—'
                Ed Hall raises his clarinet and bursts
into a wailing skipped descent of sound
and the empty saloon in Connecticut
blacks out—in a whorehouse on a riverboat
in Storeyville the grace notes tumble like a ball of glass
bouncing down a marble staircase, sharp and cracking
but not breaking quite. Filling the spaces
between his note-stream and the silence,
sizzle-sizzle-sizzle and a tump-a-tump-a
as bass and snare pace out the shifting rhythms
and now come piano chords like pilings running
out on the river beneath a pier that holds
a palace, and Kaminsky's
trumpet obligatto, muted, open,
muted, weaves the pendant pattern
of its chandeliers of sound while Edmund Hall
is leaping upward, bouncing back up up those gleaming
stairwells higher, till his slurred vibrato's
whipping down the blues arpeggio
to a clear, humming lower register so pure
it would melt the forged iron padlocks on the heart
of the attendant at Louisiana State
Hospital where Leon Rapallo,
brain gouged by syphilis, still plays
this chorus through the barred window
as the music floats off in a swirl
of motes dropping across a dusty road.
They run through 'High Society' together, each
takes a riff in turn, bold flags
of different colors spearing off
from the onward repetition of the tune,
the tune ever changing as the jam-
session opens out in all directions

till they come back
acknowledging the single tune they
sprang from, now spring out anew, in different
riffs, new sharps, new blue notes, new returns,
by some invisible bond unspoken each attuned
to the knowledge that this chorus
is stop-and-go and hence the next-to-last
before the separate wills of clarinet and brasses
—Teagarden has joined them in the midst
of all of it and launched his sliding rough
caress of sound, his tiger's love-call romping
in the cellar under sweet suspended chords and
snaffled snares and rimshots' intuitions—all
coasting through the final chorus
of 'High Society' and they reach
The End
       They take a break,

laughing, wave to the applause of couples who've arrived
in Cords and rumbleseated roadsters,
youths in ice-cream flannels, yacht-club blazers, arms
around their silky girls with the white throats and low-cut dresses,
thin wrists, the ivory cigarette-holders drooping
from long fingers, already
smashed, still in the Flaming Twenties
like the music, though it's September,
1939, and few
of us will likely make
such insouciant, plangent joy as this
in the Forties or, if we get there,
in our forties although we spend
ourselves long times from now, trying
to remember
how it was, the Picou Chorus
and the other choruses
on shining instruments that plunge
against silence, quickening
in the illusion of their absolute
freedom the yoke of only four
chords and sixteen bars, borne
so gaily by Ed Hall,
Art Hodes, Cozy Cole, Max
And Jackson T. playing our hearts out,
each in his own way, together.

At the Roman Wall, 1956

After my classes at the Faculté
I join the lonely Fulbrights. Their café
Across Rue Chabot-Charny's an oasis
In a desert of impassive faces,
An island echoing in a heedless sea.
They huddle, and their tabled ground rejoices
To the flat yammer of their American voices.
They make each other homesick, and make me.

Here in this foreign one-horse town we're far
From convivial comforts of the familiar;
It's strange, missing the reassurance latent
In mere recognition, even the blatant
Blandness of a hometown storefront street,
Here, change in the pocket's no assurance.
Taste of the bread may seem an exile's durance
And dripping beeves make one distrust one's meat.

On this café wall a plaque of bronze
Announces that these very stones were once
The Castrum Romanum's perimeter,
Marking civilization's limit, or
Were plinths for Caesar's routs beyond Dijon
(Divio, then), when this carafe's deep vintage
Was guzzled here and paid for in a mintage
Judas might have clapped his palm upon.

Here, when howling helmed Burgundians swept
Against Castrum Divionense and leapt
These battlements, the stupored Roman legions
Hightailed south toward less anarchic regions
But left their temples, stocked with gods, behind.
Here, in the shade of ruined colonial splendor
Venus' charms were hawked by the one-eyed vendor
Whose amulets for Apollo cured the blind.

Here, Saint Bénigne stumbled, speared, in chains,
His mortal heart already in high heaven,
In triumph playing Christ's agon again.
Here pilgrims trod to touch his quick remains.
Here that good Catholic Chabot-Charny scorned
An evil queen and bull of Richelieu's,
Spared Huguenots for Saint Bartholomew's
And Jesus' sakes, whose Mercy they suborned.

See, on the Place du Théatre, Rameau stands
Statue-still, who, when he waved his hands,
Brought from the lutanists' and flautists' fingers
And their breath a counterpoint that lingers
Though peruqued ladies who to his gavottes
Turned on the arms of their pomaded lovers
Like moons 'round silver planets, beneath their covers
Of weary stone sleep next the sansculottes.

Here, I drink *vin ordinaire*. The grey
Twilight throbs with old wounds. I obey
Some homing instinct, and I think of places
Where the walls change like the ever-changing faces
In a boomtown crowd, once comforting to me.
There, unbounded by old stones, our choices
Seemed self-given, and selves, like our green voices
Unresonant with echoes, sounded free.

Fontaine-les-Dijon Revisited

How could we sleep in that pension
At the foot of the hill
Below the chapel
At Fontaine-les-Dijon?

There the carillon
Shattered the stained-
Glass silence
Of our sleep.

On this high hill
Where St. Bénigne was born
A monk in the Middle Ages still
Clanged a clapper all night long

Remembering how his mother
When her term had come
Hauled her big belly
To this hill's rock dome

So her son could be birthed
Nearer heaven, so a church
In his name be erected,
His Sainthood perfected

—Speared by the Romans—
And now that this spot
Is hallowed, we dare not
Give it over to demons

Who possess the underworld
And pinch us with their spells
Unless driven back under the world
By the clang of God's bells

Which is why, at 4:30 this morning
A monk in a cassock, to mark
Each quarter-hour in the dark,
Tolls anthems fourteen minutes long

And we arise to meagre rations
Under a holy hill
Irritable as demons
Whose sleepless bed is in hell.

Reasons

Because when our clothes hung from the slanting alders
And summer the color of stream on wavering sand
Poured from the clouds, you waded under
Light-flecked glades reflected in the water
And repealed our exile from the Garden; because,
Seeing you of a sudden in the crowd
On Chestnut Street, the heedless, thoughtless plod
Of my heart was seized, and stilled, suspended
In another life, until
The beat of blood and breath resumed; because
While you're asleep the rhythm of your breathing
Sifts the air with a dark-flowered enticement;
Because when I grope through lightless labyrinths of despair
The unbroken thread of your love guides me back;
Because I cannot think of life without you
But as a season of ice and pain, of hunger
Without end; because in the candle-mold
I gave you thirty years ago, you've placed
Bouquets of pearly everlasting.

Night Fishing

You stir, or is it the first birds
Straining to open the darkness with their tongues?
You stir, you pass your arm behind my head
And we move closer, our hands find one another
As bodies slip together and thighs part—
In the dorey I bend, bend to the oars
Exultantly, bend back and the boat glides
With its wake widening behind you, and the swirled pools
The oars leave as we slash through the bold water
Where the Head of the Cape juts toward the sea.
There you cast your line—its shining lure
Arches, then trolls from the rod held in your hands
Till there's a strike—the rod bends,
You whirl the reel as the caught fish darts and turns,
Rushes the keel and the line goes slack a moment,
Then, a slash of whiteness under the gunnels
—I've shipped oars and reach for the whipping line,
At last haul out of the froth a tinker mackerel
Flashing in the fading light all sleek
Stripes and slippery frenzy—I work the hook
Out of his gaping jaw and in the bucket
Plop him with the others. Grate of shingle
Under bow, we've hauled the boat up, gathered
Driftwood sticks. In the rocky cleft our fire
Glows and our green withes of new-cut alders
Spear the cleaned meat. The sizzling drips,
Drips on the embers. On a rock of snails
We feed each other flesh with the sweet tang
Of the sea, and the fire, and salt, as the tide breathes
Its long slow breaths along the shore.
We rinse our hands and faces in a pool,
The rumpled water stills, we see ourselves
Gaze back at us among the floating stars.

Ode to Joy

Your hand trailed over the hammock's side
And like a netted mermaid, you hung in air
Lending the net the langorous shape of your
Lithe body, and the curved air
Swerved around you bearing scents
Of old shrub roses and of new-mown grass.
I sat on the steps beneath the sun that poured
On sun-filled lawn and sun-splashed holly bushes,
Sun-crested trees, magnolias afloat where sun
Like a summer shower thrust itself upon
A glimmering sea. Each new breath I drew
Was joy—I knew no name for this delight
That flowed through arteries to crest, recede,
And crest again, as endless as the tide.
The grass below was a metaphor of gladness,
The beetle underneath its blades, a trope;
The earth still damp with dew bespoke its kinship
With the linked constellations of the night.
The ivy on the wall had shone forever.
Each object of our sight, each breath
Crowded with speech this love outlasting death
That flowed through me as though it would not cease
Ever to flow, and knowing this I knew
Nothing else there was that we need know.

    That was before they pulled R. from the lake
At noon near Wilmington; before P.
Came down from the mountain, eyes glazed and mind
Blasted on LSD; that was before
G. had his stroke, then, rehabilitated,
Waited while the next stroke's fuse
Smouldered in his brain; before C.
Broke up with N., before their divorce;
Before F. grew old and grey and full of pain
And stumbled with a cane; before surgery for cancer
Left B. a little less each day; before
C's return to N. from S. and the ride
In the taxi when his heartbeat stopped and he died;
Before the wearing away and wearying of the body
As its possibilities wither and decline,

And among those present and accounted for
The obituaries in the New York Times
Feature those we knew as never before
While light seeps from a swollen sky,
Staining the foliage, the branches, the earth
Where by dint of looking I make out
A leaf, another leaf, so many leaves
Each with its own pattern of veins and greens
Hanging part of the way it hangs between
Its burst from bud and the oncome of a dry crackle
With which leaves stiffen, rub, and swirl
On the Autumn wind; by this dumb light
Shapes cast shadows and shadows grow
Until it is the twisted shades we know,
Shades that have no connection
To each other, or to the dark top hemlock bough
Where a last lone mockingbird, late straggler, pining
For the lost noon of summer, trills
His plangent repertoire, and fills
The evening air with intricate nets of sound.
Then magnolias, hemlock, hollies, eaves
Are drenched with falls of sweeter sound
Than they ever held before, as evening
Fades to dark save in the eastern sky
Where a flared moon lightens to a glow that brims,
Tinting the roofs, the tree-tops, and the ground
As though the gathered threadings of a bird's tongue
Could weave a tensile web that, hanging,
Holds the moon, and draws it up the sky.
    The very blackness of the air is laced
With light, invisible as the notes and catches
Of a moonstruck bird on a hemlock bough
Cascading from the deepest source of sorrow
To pierce the dark with momentary grace.

III

The Battle of Hastings

Schoolboys in blazers infiltrate the aisles
Of the British Museum. It's hard to read
Maps of the Battle of Hastings
While their master futilely harangues them

About the Battle of Hastings. They are intent
On tactics of their own making.
A lot they care for the plight of Harold (his forces
Bloodied and wearied from besting the Norsemen

Hundreds of miles to the north ten days before),
The Fourth Form will maintain its hegemony
Over the Third this day, come what may! At last
Their skirmish deploys through doorways, advancing

Into the Hall of Clocks. Another batallion
In blazers—maroon, not green—troops through the Map Room
Scuffling, and out, save for one laggard, a toddler
But three feet tall. He can't even see into the cases.

His head is large, his legs and arms are stubby and bent,
His steps necessarily small. And now two boys
In green for some reason retrace their steps,
Sniffling. Down the center aisle, they catch a glimpse

Of maroon, the enemy color, and rush
To opposite sides of the hall. They have him
Cornered!—then see he's not a mere babe in Infants, but their age,
A midget-sized monster providentially provided

For their satisfaction. He watches the boy at one end
Of the aisle, sees the eyes gleam, the curled lip
Of one waiting for him to come nearer. He turns
And at the other end of the aisle, sees

The other, lip curled and eyes eager to torment him.
He suddenly ducks under the cases, bobs up in the next aisle
But they move over an aisle and are waiting as before.
He is trapped, there is no escaping

Being born to endure the revenge of unknown adversaries
For an offense of which he must be innocent
Except for being born. I saw the terror
In that boy's face, and the desperate resolve

To run, or if he couldn't, then to do
His poor best for honor's sake
And not go down snivelling beneath the blows
Of the always larger, stronger. This was one

Battle in a series already long that might
Be averted—*'Young man,'* I said, *'I'm lost—*
Perhaps you can show me the way out?'
And so let him lead me to safety

Through his enemies, as though there is
A way out. In the entrance hall, surprised
By what they see beside me, others turn
With heedless stare and curious intent;

He pretends he doesn't notice them.
I thank him. I must go. The lines
Are being drawn. Among the columns
He appraises his next defensive position.

Witnesses

No witnesses. Nobody driving
At 80 mph happened to notice why
This yellow Chevy with the West Virginia plates
Swerved out on the shoulder, then careened, rolling
Over and over, ending upside-
Down, the four wheels spinning, clutching
At the clouds and the roof crushed,
The highway spattered with splintered
Windows and the sun staining
Rainbows in oilslick—

By the time the first few travellers stopped
And got out of their cars and other
Speeding cars gaping through
Their windows slowed down to a crawl
They had managed somehow to crawl
Out of the wreck, and just lay there,
All but one, perhaps the driver,
Staggering up and down the gulley
Stunned, bleeding—

The baby with a pulsing welt
Matting its silky hair, the blood
Rising and sinking from the fontanelle
In the rhythm of a rapid heartbeat,
Gasping and bawling, now gathered in the huge
Enclosing arms of the grandmother who sits
With her eyes closed by the roadside, rocking,
Crooning, rocking—

The mother flat on her back in the dusty rut,
Her bruised eyes darkening with blood,
Blood trickling from her ear,
Trickling in a dark seam that falls
In droplets gleaming in the dust like engine oil,
Her hands pale, feebly groping, her shallow calling
'My baby . . . My baby . . . '

Her husband coming to his senses, losing now
The merciful oblivion of shock,
Staggering up from the gulley, seeing now
The consequences of a moment's error, unbelieving,
Gapes at where she lies there on the ground, bleeding,
Now believing hurls himself upon her
To squeeze her broken ribs in his embrace,

His voice of a wounded grizzly howling, sobbing
'My wife . . . My wife . . . My wife . . . '
It took the four of us to wrestle him,
To hold him to the ground with hammerlocks,
With imprecations and the empty consolations,
The rude inadequate attempts of strangers
To give assurances while witnessing
Disaster—

The lines of slowed-down speeders crawled along
In both directions, cars backed up in rows,
Faces pressed against the windows feasting
On this tableau as though provided
To appease their hunger for disaster,
Watching the smashed car, baby bleeding,
Mother now unconscious and the father
Sobbing hysterically in our arms so close,
So slow, they could reach out and touch him
Yet distanced behind glass, their eyes
Fixed on the scene as on a screen,
A picture of a real disaster
Somehow not real—

The farmer who had climbed his fence was saying
'If she don't make it there that'll be nineteen
Gone since Eighty-One was opened.'
His wife has called the sheriff. When
Will the sheriff come, the ambulance
Bring help? The single strand
Of telephone line swings from the farmhouse,
Sags between diminished poles toward town . . .
Over the hilltop flash the bloodshot eye-
Winks atop the police car's shrill annunciation
Staining the valley, now the deeper klaxon
Of ambulance howls toward us, brakes

Screech, doors swing open, stretchers
Slide, the crew is lifting—*Easy! . . . Easy there . . .* —the injured in,
Slam shut,
They're off with siren
Growling, as it rises growing faint,
The hilltop bloodlight humps and winks its last—

The sheriff's aide is sweeping broken glass.
The cars now barely slow down as they pass.
What earthly good did we do here, stunned
By the pain of strangers, but as witnesses aware
Of the doom that hovers blind in the guileless air—
Back in our cars, engines turned on again,
We secure our seat-belts and move on
Toward our own
Destinations.

Jogger

Entered in an event
For which he hasn't trained,

His body is pushing beyond
The limits of the body:

That flat, muscular stomach
So many sit-ups drew taut

(But his sweatsuit is shredded by moths)
Swags over his belt in a bulge.

And what's going on with his features?
They each have a will of their own.

They've decided they're not fully grown,
They're getting too big for themselves—

The nose is thicker, the skin
On the chin wants to hang, so hangs down.

And the face is creased and padded
In a parcel of furrows and folds.

Somewhere under addenda
Of belly and rump and jowl

Strides the crisp youth and slender
Who used to run a quick mile

As if he were still the same
Though what he ran toward became him.

He's within hail of the finish,
His record is writ in flesh.

Crack!

What was that?—The crack of doom or a sonic boom,
Bursting gas main or exploding furnace? A bomb
Set by guerillas mistaking the corner mailbox
For a pillar of the Military-Industrial Complex?

That tremor assaulting the soundtrack of silent dream
Only jostled the sharp night air. The dishes' rattling
Stopped before I had stifled my stifled scream
Or had the light on, or my mind working.

My wife switches the dark back on. We slip from shock
To sleep while deep below us, rigid rock
Blocks the insensate seethe at the core—We wake,
Only our curtains move, and the wind in the lindens.

Slick

Despite strangulated cries
Of dune-lovers and the bourgeoisie
In coastal resorts, thirsty

Turbines, trucks, tractors, cars,
Furnaces, hair-groom sets and
Electric toothbrushes demand

Minarets on stilts offshore,
Steel straws shoved down
Through chocolate mud. The juice

Pulses faster than the earth's
Hind tit will serve us, oozing
Through faults in beds of shale

To blacktop surface waves
Where downed gulls
Make no departures.

By unseasonable gale
Pitched shoreward, oil
Casts trouble on troubled waters.

A slithering sauce fouls
Nests the waves pound.
Fish float belly-up,

The earth is bleeding.
An ocean of salt
Rubs in our wounds.

Mother

Mother whose breasts were our green mountains
And whose assuring breath was scented summer air,

Whose body was the fields, the mounds, the valleys
It was our fortune to explore,

What happened? Your teeming valleys
Erupt in rash wounds, gashes. From sores

Vile fumes deaden the leaves. We are bequeathed
Your proud flesh, your powdered milk-of-ashes.

Scrolls from the Dead

We already had some gospels, when he fell
Into a cave of potsherds and a screed
Tattered by beetles, half-unreadable.
Years to break the cipher. Who had need
Of his long, earpulled labors, all to eke
Unknown annunciations into a guise
Of English?—'From golden meekness may the meek
Inherit meekness. Unfallen, the mighty rise.
Birds shall nest in the dust, and lay stones.'

Why couldn't he let us go about our business,
The mighty guzzling at their bar of brass,
The meek weaned on the skimmed milk of meekness
As fewer birds return each Spring, our solace
An old tale of the breath that stirs the bones?

Halflives

After the third day ash began to sift
Like snow in a bottle on the steepled town
—Or, to be precise, on steeples' stumps.
A crust formed on the mud caked where the shore was.
Then dark rains turned this matter spongeish. No
Tale of ancient wanderers' travails
Conceived a Nature so intolerant:
Daylong the hot winds howl, by dark drear sludge
And ruins melded into foetid clay,
Leafless, no bird riffling the unshadowed sky—
Deep in the bunkhouse, canned food almost gone,
His eye at the eyepiece of the periscope
Fixed on the shore . . . the spongey mass turns mauve,
Takes shapes like mouth-like algae eating one another,
Seeps to shore, spreads tendrils, stretches tubes
Or stems that ooze out jellied leaves. 'All clear,'
He thinks not speaking lest he break the quiet
Now after the first delivery.
The final bulb grows dimmer, then flicks out.
She hasn't wakened from her deep sleep yet
At her breast it grubs, twitching all its claws.

The Finish

The first runner reached us
bearing the news before
he was expected by
the camera crews—the instant
replay showed him strolling
by the roadside, sucking
half an orange. Who'd think
he had endured so many
miles? They demanded
he re-run the final
fifty yards while they
re-filmed him. While they filmed him
a second runner crossed
the line but by the time
the cameras turned to him
the second runner wasn't
running any longer
but sucking half an orange;
he too must re-enact
the second finish, since
the public is entitled
to the real thing.
Just as he re-crossed
the line, finishing second
a second time, here comes
puffing up the hill
the third man, at his heels
the crazy crowd the first
runner came to tell of
but had no chance to tell
anyone while cameras
caught his second first
finish and then turned
from him and scanned the second
finish of the second
finisher, the spent
third man with an orange
in his hand, the raggle-
taggle mob arriving
at the reviewing stand,

and soon there's blood all over
the finish line and no
reviewers and no stand,
but what viewer could
believe this, cameras still
following the third
man suck his orange? The crews
urge the crowd once more
to re-enact the finish—

IV

David's Folly

The town was famous then, though few recall
When the seven Tapley brothers sailed the seas,
Each captain of a vessel named to please
A girl back here, to whom he'd tell his tall
And hair's-breadth tales of heathen, rock, and squall . . .
How many yearned for the rush of an offshore breeze;
But most stayed home, to plant and pick their peas,
Cut hay, wood, stone, ice, and haul
What they had cut: lives measured by the rod.
Their boast, how big their barns—till David Wasson
Outbuilt all with his 'Folly'; who knew here trod
An unsung Psalmist, chores his orison,
Who scorched *The Dial* with diatribes on God
And wrote two poems that once pleased Emerson?

Great Owl

After the echo of your flight
The trees' sighing
And the chittering fields
Are shushed now
As by snowfall
In ghostlight.

What moves in the shadow
Of your cry?
Locked in stone,
Mammoth bones stir,
The charred sticks
Of dead fires glow.

A Stillness

Each bead of the mist is burning
with the joy
of a resurrected soul.

A will within it
draws it back from me a little—the cove,
a beach of shallow pools
behind the sandbars, and the bay
without motion
blending, somewhere
into the fog, the infinite empire
of floating fiery light.

Alone,
tracing the cove that curves
like a breast and slowly fills
the shrinking beach with light

a heron
stalks. She stands

on one leg very still, for a long time.

The blade of her beak
jabs
—water breaks and the speared minnow flashes in air,
is swallowed before
I can be sure
she has moved at all.

A ripple spreads its dying rings.

She has been given
an invisible sign,
she reaches out great wings and launches
into slow deliberate flight, trailing
legs like reeds,
thrusting the serpent's curve of throat
toward the all-consuming light

where earth melts into water,
water into air and the air
is alive with fire—

She's gone, leaving a stillness where I
breathe in
a savage calm beyond desire.

That Morning

Look, he's let the kitchen fire go out
You said. Not in the house, the barn, the yard—
Going on fourteen, I said. It will go hard
With him he's such a lazy, shiftless lout.
High time he did his chores. I raised a shout
Flinging his name across the fields toward
The cliff . . . only a broken echo jarred
The long silence with its stabbing doubt.

What if I hadn't, when we turned to leave
The farm that morning as they pecked our corn
Said I'd give a penny for each dead crow
I thought—and rushed to where the fence was torn:
A boy crossed barbed wire, pulled his shotgun through
Till trigger caught, and the years are ours to grieve.

Old Reprobate

Old son, he said
When the fifth was nearly dead,
Your eyes look tired
As a dog's
Pee-holes in the snow.

One time the snow crews
Wouldn't clear his road
So he shaped him snowshoes
Like a bear's paws.
Where they'd plough, he strode—

It's been eleven years
And the snow crew still
Sees bear
In the woods, the brush,
Everywhere.

He'd say, I remember
Standing, as a kid
On that beach, holding
The horse's head
With the tide away out

And the rocks all rattling,
Sounded like a dancer
With castanets and heels
At the edge of the water
And Father pulling

The rockweed back,
Pitchforking lobsters
From every crack.
They'd twist like eels
Piled high on our waggon,

So many we'd strew
Them like manure
To make the corn grow.
On a still afternoon
I used to row

At halftide to the ledges,
Muffled oars,
Injun-like, slow,
Sneak up and grab me
A seal or two—

You ever tried
Seal steak, Dan?
Delicious, fried.
—But now
The seals are few,

Lobster's scarce,
There's been no bears
In a dozen years.
He's the game warden
And our fifth is gone.

Last Lynx

A census of murdered
Chickens. Entrails and bones
Swarming with green
And blue bottle-flies,
An incriminating scene

Like hound-dogs slashed,
Bellies gashed open,
The guts dragged
Howling a little ways
Towards home—

Who'd need to see half
A footprint in soft
Earth after rain,
It was the last
Lynx in Hancock County

And they all went
Out on that hunt,
For the fun, the excitement,
Some for the bounty.
With their shot-guns and deer-guns

They blazed at anything moving.
Those damned fools near killed
Their sons, their companions.
Never got near her.
She's gone,

Leaving the legends
Of her crafty will
And the longings of hunters
As keen as the hungers
She sates with her kill.

At Don's Garage

He ought to be hung.

But don't bother to call
the warden or sheriff,
they're of no use,
no use at all

since nobody actually saw
him, in rank midsummer, draw
a bead on that moose
—rotten shot, hit her in the shoulder—
nobody watched
as he didn't follow
to finish her off
where she thrashed,
blood pumping out of her side,
clots of red on her hide,
on the hardhack, the ground,
a trail wobbling back
through Camp Stream Swamp

till you don't need your eyes
to find her
belly bulged big as a balloon
nostrils noisy with flies
and a dead stench smothering
wild roses and the trumpet vine,

but some of us think we know
—we think of who we think shot that doe
and her fawn out of season
last month, and not for meat,
left them dead in the woods
just for the hell of it

—now would there be two like that in the same county?—

but if you haven't seen the deed, they say
it just don't signify. No way
you can testify against him.

You can only curse him.

Don called him a rottenlivered sonovabitch.

Virgil called him a yellowbellied bastard and made
reference to several serious defects
in his ancestry and breeding.

Bink called on God to pour
brushkiller in his beer.

We called on his chainsaw to jump
clear of the stump
and take his leg off,

we called on Camp Stream Swamp
to open its peat bog to his tread
and let him slide in the water and under the leafslime
up to his shoulders, his chin, his head,
let him holler awhile as he thrashes around
and gurgle then for a time
till the swampwater is still

except for the skeeters and whirligigs dancing
in the evening, when bullfrogs and peepers resume
the high tones and low sounds
of their old duet.

Ants

Theirs is a perfection of pure form.
Nobody but has his proper place and knows it.
Everything they do is functional.
Each foray in a zigzag line
Each prodigious lifting
Of thirty-two times their own weight
Each excavation into the earth's core
Each erection
Of a crumbly parapetted tower—

None of these feats is a private pleasure,
None of them done
For the sake of the skill alone—

They've got a going concern down there,
A full egg-hatchery
A wet-nursery of aphids
A trained troop of maintenance engineers
Sanitation experts
A corps of hunters
And butchers
An army

A queen.
Each
Is nothing without the others, each being a part
Of something greater than all of them put together
A purpose which none of them knows
Since each is only
The one thing that he does. There is
A true consistency
Toward which their actions tend.
The ants have bred and inbred to perfection.
The strains of their genes that survive survive.
Every possible contingency
Has been foreseen and written into the plan.

Nothing they do will be wrong.

Lines for Scott Nearing

(1883–1983)

And what if you were wrong about Albania?
You called child labor Capitalism's disease
While children toiled in the coalmines of Trustees
Of the University of Pennsylvania,
Who fired you from their Wharton School forthwith—
A *cause célèbre*! Our tenured free speech grew
Out of 'the Nearing case.' But not for you,
Old rebel loner, bound to Reason's myth—
The economy is just that is all planned.
Was this what in your old age drew the young
To your walled garden, as witness to a life
Of Thoreau's abnegations, though with a wife?
Your rows of Escarole, Romaine, Deer's Tongue
—How comely, how proportionate your land.

A Felled Tree

When the sky stopped glowering and glazed hailstones
shrank from ice-eggs to dull pebbles in puddles,

when winds that wrenched leaf-heavy heads of maples
in our grove roared off toward other trees

and the great limbs cracked and boughs crashed down,
when the tree split open, the trunk revealed

how it had stood held upright by its rind.
Heartwood spewed out of the stump

in crumbled profusion, a richer earth
than that from which it grew. Three barrowfuls

we spread around the boxwood. I'd be
disciple to a felled tree, if it could tell

how the soil my days are rooted in
can, at the core of me, be mulched

into a finer stuff than I have touched,
compact, and dark as humus is,

nourishing another life
yet redolent of this.

V

Words

I will commit
no longer poems to suffer
the Chinese water torture
of the iamb, will not rhyme
at any time nor think but seek
and speak the gutreaction poem
of the soul's discovering
it is a soul the id-
entity poem
that grows like roots
stalks leaves petals flesh
poems belly poems thigh
poems of the erogenous
response poems to you
poems that are themselves the
sound of your
slip rustling and the
scent that laces
the air you wear and breathing
this I rummage with a secret
purpose among heaped and hoarded
words spilling from the battered
chests in my attic and see
they shake themselves free
from lint and dust they
form in comely clusters moving
by their own mysterious
will through louvered windows
out toward the meadow caressing
the bulged curving
fenders of parked cars and
stony paths and scrub pines
and thistles by the ledges holding
their folded and unfolding
wings of cabbage butterflies
in motions
like those the scent or sound made
that aroused them and now
they approach you and you
are the landscape

of their native country,
they know they need no longer
search or wander
they surrender
everything they carried
on their journey becoming
just what they dreamed of
becoming. Goodby, words. They
do become you. I've
no more to say.

Problems of Knowledge

[The Phi Beta Kappa Poem
College of William and Mary, 1974]

What do you really know? I asked, phrasing the question
in Words. But what are Words? replied that circuit in the Mind
plugged in as Answer Desk; then, as the line went dead
Concatenation jostled Games, and tinkling Symbol
made such a racket who could hear Communication?
Each had a proposition. Have you ever
Heard the uproar of your whole vocabulary
yelling at once, each word a keening sibyl
confiding its wise counsels to the wind's ear?
Madness! And when you harken to the few of them
who get through the general donnybrook, what do *they* know?
Contradiction pounds the gavel while Ambiguity
argues that Answer's only half a pair of twins.
A lot of good that does. Then the Monosyllables
Love   Woe   Hate   and Hope
each full of herself arise to sing an aria
against the orchestrated din and hubbub.
My head is splitting. How can I make this rabble
of prophets subside in silence if not in agreement?
—There must be something they can all assent and shut up to.
Harmony, what do you say? Cacophony's splenetic
coughing skewers your sweet chords. O Folly, Folly,
this must be all your doing. Myself, where are you?
What have you done, what have *I* done, unloosing
these monstrous egotists, each the protagonist
of a total epic, an untranslatable spell—
What did you say? They are all heroes? Each lives
in his own consciousness of my knowing
the myths tolled in his syllables, the sound of his name
incising a verse of the race's history
in the near-blank tablets of my mind—

it must be so, it was said to me by Mind,
Tablets, History, Sound, and Spell
in those very words, or in so many words.

Essay on Style

Announced himself Autocrat of all.
All he could grab was his,
Astonishment also. He invoked the
Abecedary of his affections.
Articulation became the purpose of all his study.
Arcana he resurrected and put to uses only
Adepts could recognize, yet everyone must
Acknowledge his originality, if not his power, his charm.

But by then he'd become
Bored and decided that he'd
Begin again, this time by
Boring from within
But found the behests he would turn on themselves
Already contained their own
Abnegations so he cut that out and soon
Began again: The problem was to find what
Belonged to anyone but had not yet
Been recognized. What to do? He
Brandished bucolics as his own invention, juxtaposed to the
Barbarous in bold combinations;
Banishment from joy he
Broadcast as the soul's estate until he
Bequeaths it joy. Blood spurts with the heart-
Beat of his declamations! What he
Borrows becomes his estate. He
Bewilders the uninitiate with his bounty,
Beggaring most of his imitators.

But he
Concluded at last he would
Close out this line of
Bagatelles, tired ballads, the old
Bardic strut.
Accomplishment demanded something else, like
Allegory, for starters, or
Archetypes, but they'd been done. He'd settle,
Certain of his rightness, for his own
Caprices and therefore preached
Canons of celebration,
Cloudy yet coherent, a cryptic

Concord that subsumed condemnations.
Chorales of his made cunning
Contact with much of the universe.
Crooked, contrary, and cruel are his captives,
Coral and chrysoprase among his colors. The
Curious have enhanced his reputation.

Dull did he find this in time, though,
Daring to demand then a
Deckchair in which to do his own dreams.
Almost all of the chairs were
Bulging with
Characters whose names in
Any old order
Began to comprise a
Convention of the Great, the Nearly-Great, the not-so-great, the
Copiers and carboncopiers of copies,
Anthologizers, neologizers, those who
Breathed, gasped, howled, sang, stuttered in
Committees, many of them hung up on forms of
Address long familiar, others
Adept at arcana no longer arcane or
Borrowers bringing together their
Cracked reproductions of chunks of the
Chaos as though imitation
Comprised creation—His restless
Daemon declares independence from that lot.
Dictates from the deity within him, his
Destiny, directs that he now
Discover the drift of his difference. What in these
Days of disjunction endures? A
Diction to say
Desire, dawn, death, despair, descant,
Direct disclosures in dextrous dirges,
Devour, depart, dig, digress, discard and discord
—Doggone, it's a domain here a man can
Do or die in, go
Daft with the delicacy and the daring, the
Dazzle of dew in the darkness—let his
Doodlings disclose new delights, for this dialect
Defies desolation.
                    Eager, explores that

Elysian empire where
Entire concatenations of vocables,
English, will do his bidding in
Fables, in phrases, in forms and
Felicitous figures, as long as that grand
Gaullimaufry, the Lexicon, bids all his doings. But
How can this or any part of this
Happen unless
He has enticed
Her, his heedless
Headstrong Muse?
He will seek till he find her,
He will climb over ledges of syntactical terrain,
Hacking through thickets of thought,
He'll grope past the dolmens of his despair till
He comes, at the summit, to her
Hostel of all delights. With
Her by his side, with
Her blessing, he'll
Hover, he'll swoop, and soar,
Hang-gliding from Helicon, over the world.

Crossing Walt Whitman Bridge

Walt, my old classmates who write poems
Have written poems to you.
They find you, old fruit,

In the supermarket, California;
They hear you speaking from the brazen mouth
Of your statue on Bear Mountain

In poems, so many poems—
You are large, you can contain them.
From my Philadelphia suburb I drive across

Walt Whitman Bridge
Into the freedom of New Jersey,
Passing the Walt Whitman Bar & Grill,

Walt Whitman Auto Parts & Junk Yard, Whitman
Theatre, Whitman Motor Inn,
Your Pharmacy, your Package Store,

Your Body Shop,
And yes,
Your supermarket's really in New Jersey!

Past old bottles, fenders, corrugated shacks,
Your neon name on mirrored doors
And winos slumped across the stoops

Shadowed by the boarded thirteen-storey
Walt Whitman Hotel no longer glutted
With Americans who'd never read a line of yours,

Speeding now, I think of you
Ingesting science, scent of haybarns, daily news and country bunkum
To translate the Farmer's Almanac into a Jeremiad

And mix the sinner's Presbyterian dreams into your cockalorum
(You Nosey Parker, peeping through the transom
Of his relentless dream),

To make the murmuration of crowds
Into leaves of compassion—
What you spit out

Would keep all Europe
Civilized two thousand years!
What have you left but

A larger continent
Bulging to belch and yawp, lusting
For the nightwind's breast, the curled

Lascivious kisses
Of the frondy sea? Approaching
Mannahatta (it waits

Where the road dips far ahead
Beyond the toll-booths and the tunnel,
Spires rising to jostle the horizon

Over fumes and loud arrivals,
The press of crowds as in the old days)
I think of you—prodigious

Your digestion, swallowing
Democracy, not flinching from the secret
Shame exposed by torchlit nightmare,

The drowned swimmer and the battle-death—
All the heroes! Pocahantas too!
A letch for handsome draymen,

Ecstasy in capillaries
As in turning stars—How did you
Rise through itches from the bed

You and your idiot brother
Shared in a drunken
Father's house, your flabby body

Indolently moving
Toward the lightning's revelation,
Fecundity sanspareil!

It wasn't easier before the advent
Of a landscape gouged for money
Or the coming down of fallout

Than now after the dismantling
Of the brave *Bonne Homme Richard*
And the end of horsecars

To plant your seed
In Death's eyesocket
There to sprout in

Visionary life,
Always resurgent,
Never held down for long,

Felt alive,
Conceived and spoken,
So made true.

Mark Twain, 1909

. . . his hair an aureole, white
cloud around a face half
eclipsed in shadow—*'Everyone
is a moon, and has a dark
side he never shows
to anybody'*—in his white
suit, Palm Beach white, white
cravat, the eyes like cinders
gazing on devastation
past Mr. Amy crouched
beneath his black sheet, peering
toward the future. Behind him,
in the bookcase, only one
title in focus, thick book:
THE NILE. Always rivers,
rivers, the mind afloat on
currents, eddies . . . Memory
the raft that bears us onward,
onward, back to our threatened
Paradise, the waters
rising, where sounds of evening
—hoot owl, a barking dog—
are harbingers of death. It's
death that makes the present
ache so for the past, as
time that won't be stilled
swirls us toward an end we
cannot grasp. Like shadows
our story lengthens, lengthens
behind us. As Amy squeezes
the bulb, from the next room
—*'Youth!'*—Livy calls, he
starts, and this sitting
for the photograph is ended.

A Letter to W. H. Auden

Swarthmore, Pennsylvania

When the Romantic Ego had begun to fester
In the junkyard of its own corroded trophies
    —Shattered discs of Traubel in *The Ring*,
        Guns as obsolescent as the dragon,
            And piles of gold
Hoarded from teeth once filled by dentists in Berlin—

Some of us followed *maquis* in the liberation
Of the line from meters; other columns fought
    For freedom from dictatorships of logic
        Or purged their poems of lust for country lanes.
            But none prevailed
As did the Seeker in the land that never rains

Where our each loveless woe has been foretold and quoted
And footnoted, while bells toll on empty pews. That's how
    It was, when you came from your distant home,
        Abandoned mineshafts, rivers flowing North,
            And ancient rhythms
On the tongue. Across the border you stepped forth

From the nursery to schoolboy games, already
Armed with tricks and spells enough to stand the hairdos
    Of our Enemies on end. There, sly
        Error, in a fashionable skin
            —Already splitting—
Becomes a newer creature even as the eye

Takes in its form, and by its form is taken in.
But none of Error's writhing heads knows what defences
    Could hold at bay the Hero of that Quest
        Whose end is with the honest Truth's reflection
            To jest and dazzle,
Then, with wit's quick strokes, lop off each one. Correction:

You made the near-perfection of your art reproach
For its botched work the slothful heart, under-achiever.
    Just down the street from my house stands the mock-
    Venetian villa with its tower, where
        You parsed and graded
Laborious compositions by the Chinese Air

Cadets and explications by indigenous
Co-eds whose children read you in my seminars.
> There you found a tongue for Caliban,
> There wrote of villagers who wouldn't see
>> The unicorn
In their azaleas—yet still speak of that Englishman

Who shuffled in to dinner at the Ingleneuk
His feet in carpet slippers!—But of course you knew
> How Life, *l'homme moyen sensuel*, recalls
> The grace of vision as oddness of dress.
>> For 'Poetry
Makes nothing happen'—that is, nothing more, or less,

Than how we see reality. Now how we act,
That's our affair, not Poetry's; no use to hold
> The poem responsible for what the reader
> To whom its home truths bring the invitation,
>> *Change your life!*
Does with his life. Enough, that in the ordination

Of your language—alliteration, zeugma, trope—
The blade of rectitude is sheathed in our delight.
> Those forms of feeling breathing in the forms
> Of verse resuscitate, in these dark days,
>> Us who receive
Your gifts and offer you our gratitude, our praise.

Her Obedient Servant

(Robert Graves, 1895–1985)

He ferreted first things to their first cause:
The Alphabet, to trees in a Sacred Grove;
The one true theme of poetry, to love
Under the immitigable Muse's laws,

Her laws all else is lost for if obeyed,
Ardor inseparable from primal fright
As when bombardment raked his trench all night
And Reason gibbered in a world gone mad.

His gift was twinned, as he himself was twain—
His suppliant lover's, his strict captain's art
Found bliss and death clutched one to the other's heart,
For simple Truth with Paradox had lain.

His poems, spurning the chaos of our days,
On passion shed their coruscating blaze
As, at the instant of the year's ascension,
Stonehenge's heelstone pours the blinding sun.

Reflections

Consider: the mind's a mirror of
the world. The land we seek, of houses
more comely than our house is, yet
familiar, beckons in a glass
that holds all images in light
clearer than the day's. But where
do glimmering mirrors find the shapes
they clarify? An eye that gazes
upwards holds only reflections,
dazzling, of the unformed sky.
Should what we inherit gleam
like townscapes in a slanting light,
all that we are and could become
stands evident as architecture.
But should that orchard be hewn down,
the known town razed, the wrecker's ball
hurled at walls of memory's house,
how then recompose the ruin?
The world's a mirror of the mind.

Disorder casts disorder's shadow.
What image is there but reflects
the character of its conceiver
as though our genes spawned in the womb
heroic gestures, beauty's fads,
our courtesies, the routes of trade,
spires, the secret rites of love?
As though it's in our blood, not in
cuneiform or the extraction
of ferrous metals nor contrivance
of the aerofoil. What bears our
lives through scathing space but time
unending and our own tenacious,
vulnerable selves: the clocks
dying on the wall between
their weekly windings, and the squirmy
plasm living till its needed
and annunciatory hour?
I'd melt the shadow from these things:

That continuity is blessed
whose image moves in endless change,
whose largesse can transfigure all
that must have lain in muck, in dirt,
in root. Consider interactions
of rain and soil, of fact and myth,
of flesh that perishes in time
conceiving life, making the world
the mind discovers in reflection
a reality held hidden till
created by the dying cells
of mind revealing what is there
in the forms it is not here in
unless by mind's enunciation.
Our joy is truthful fallacy.
Our final city will perfect
its own impermanent reflection,
this silver solipsism shining
behind the mirror as before.